Honor Killings

Other Books of Related Interest

At Issue Series

Gender Politics
Islamic Fundamentalism
Women in Islam

Current Controversies Series

Family Violence
Pakistan
Violence Against Women

Opposing Viewpoints Series

Gendercide
Religion and Sexuality
Women's Health

GLOBALVIEWPOINTS

Honor Killings

Lisa Idzikowski, Book Editor

GREENHAVEN
PUBLISHING

Published in 2018 by Greenhaven Publishing, LLC
353 3rd Avenue, Suite 255, New York, NY 10010

Cover image: Arif Ali/AFP/Getty Images
Maps: frees/Shutterstock.com

Library of Congress CataloginginPublication Data

Names: Idzikowski, Lisa, editor.
Title: Honor killings / Lisa Idzikowski, book editor.
Other titles: Global viewpoints.
Description: New York, NY : Greenhaven Publishing, 2018. | Series: Global
  viewpoints | Includes bibliographical references and index. | Audience: Grades 9-
  12.
Identifiers: LCCN 2017016484| ISBN 9781534501331 (library bound) | ISBN
  9781534501317 (pbk.)
Subjects: LCSH: Honor killings. | Women--Violence against. | Women--Crimes
  against. | Women's rights--Islamic countries.
Classification: LCC HV6250.4.W65 H655 2018 | DDC 306.87--dc23
LC record available at https://lccn.loc.gov/2017016484

Manufactured in the United States of America

Website: http://greenhavenpublishing.com

Contents

Chapter 2: The Cultural Origins of Honor Killing

Chapter 3: Violence Against Women Is on the Rise Worldwide

Chapter 4: What Can Be Done About Honor Killing?

Foreword

"The problems of all of humanity can
only be solved by all of humanity."
—*Swiss author Friedrich Dürrenmatt*

Global interdependence has become an undeniable reality. Mass media and technology have increased worldwide access to information and created a society of global citizens. Understanding and navigating this global community is a challenge, requiring a high degree of information literacy and a new level of learning sophistication.

Building on the success of its flagship series, Opposing Viewpoints, Greenhaven Publishing has created the Global Viewpoints series to examine a broad range of current, often controversial topics of worldwide importance from a variety of international perspectives. Providing students and other readers with the information they need to explore global connections and think critically about worldwide implications, each Global Viewpoints volume offers a panoramic view of a topic of widespread significance.

Drugs, famine, immigration—a broad, international treatment is essential to do justice to social, environmental, health, and political issues such as these. Junior high, high school, and early college students, as well as general readers, can all use Global Viewpoints anthologies to discern the complexities relating to each issue. Readers will be able to examine unique national perspectives while, at the same time, appreciating the interconnectedness that global priorities bring to all nations and cultures.

Material in each volume is selected from a diverse range of sources, including journals, magazines, newspapers, nonfiction books, speeches, government documents, pamphlets, organization newsletters, and position papers. Global Viewpoints is truly global, with material drawn primarily from international sources available in English and secondarily from US sources with extensive international coverage.

Features of each volume in the Global Viewpoints series include:

- An **annotated table of contents** that provides a brief summary of each essay in the volume, including the name of the country or area covered in the essay.

- An **introduction** specific to the volume topic.

- For each viewpoint, an **introduction** that contains notes about the author and source of the viewpoint explains why material from the specific country is being presented, summarizes the main points of the viewpoint, and offers three **guided reading questions** to aid in understanding and comprehension.

- **For further discussion** questions that promote critical thinking by asking the reader to compare and contrast aspects of the viewpoints or draw conclusions about perspectives and arguments.

- A worldwide list of **organizations to contact** for readers seeking additional information.

- A **periodical bibliography** for each chapter and a **bibliography of books** on the volume topic to aid in further research.

- A comprehensive **subject index** to offer access to people, places, events, and subjects cited in the text.

Global Viewpoints is designed for a broad spectrum of readers who want to learn more about current events, history, political science, government, international relations, economics, environmental science, world cultures, and sociology—students doing research for class assignments or debates, teachers and faculty seeking to supplement course materials, and others wanting to understand current issues better. By presenting how people in various countries perceive the root causes, current consequences, and proposed solutions to worldwide challenges, Global Viewpoints volumes offer readers opportunities to enhance their global awareness and their knowledge of cultures worldwide.

Introduction

> *"Every year around the world an increasing number of women are reported killed in the name of 'honor.' Relatives, usually male, commit acts of violence against wives, sisters, daughters and mothers to reclaim their family honor from real or suspected actions that are perceived to have compromised it.*
>
> *So-called honor killings are based on the deeply rooted belief that women are objects and commodities, not human beings entitled to dignity and rights equal to those of men."*
> —Amnesty International

Honor killing is a label given to a special type of violence committed against women. *Merriam-Webster* defines honor killing as "the traditional practice in some countries of killing a family member who is believed to have brought shame on the family." While the *Oxford English Dictionary* explains it as "the killing of a relative, especially a girl or woman, who is perceived to have brought dishonour on the family."

Also referred to as honor-based violence or honor crimes, honor killing is most prevalent in Middle Eastern, South Asian, and North African countries—including Pakistan, India, Jordan, Afghanistan, Turkey and Yemen—but is sadly frequent in the West as well. The common denominator among all these disparate regions is the institution of patriarchy, which expects and encourages fathers or other male relatives to be dominant and in control of female relatives. Women and girls are taught from very young ages that they are inferior to men and must obey their male relatives at all times or face strict censure and consequences.

Patriarchal societies—which exist in tribal communities as well as urban "modern" ones—frequently include marriage rituals which demand that women be virtuous and pure. If women or girls are suspected of losing their virtue—be it in the form of their physical virginity or their theoretical moral fiber—they are seen as bringing shame or dishonor upon their families.

Culpable behavior that casts a non-virtuous shadow "can range from talking with an unrelated male to consensual sexual relations outside marriage to being a victim of rape to seeking a divorce or refusing to marry the man her family has chosen for her," according to Amnesty International. Wearing makeup or revealing clothing, or even staying up late, can also constitute shameful behavior. Girls are raised with one role in mind, to preserve their family's honor, while boys are taught that as men they must ensure that female relatives do not injure familial honor. Offending women suffer grave consequences—which often means death at the hands of male relatives. Incredibly, the perpetrators see themselves as doing no wrong. In fact they are proud of their actions and claim it as their duty, proclaiming that the act of killing reinstates familial honor and standing in their communities.

An estimated five thousand deaths caused by honor killings occur worldwide each year, and experts say that this number may be startlingly low because most deaths go unrecorded—reported as accidents or suicides and therefore not categorized as honor killings.

People in the West typically believe that these crimes happen elsewhere, but there is ample evidence that honor killings are on the rise in parts of Europe as well as the United States and Canada. Many human rights organizations and feminist groups argue that domestic violence perpetuated in Western countries is also a form of honor-based abuse. According to the Canadian Department of Justice, "The magnitude of honour killings in Canada is largely unknown, but there are anecdotal reports about its occurrence. Such occurrences often relate to specific cultural communities where some immigrants to Canada had maintained cultural practices from their country of origin."

Countries affected by these emerging trends of violence are having difficulty dealing with the crimes. Some are attempting to enact laws they hope will discourage wrongdoing, but in some instances authorities are reluctant to act for fear of setting off cultural landmines.

Education on, and awareness of, this troubling cycle of violence is just one small step on the path to eradicating honor killings. The articles in *Global Viewpoints: Honor Killings* shine a light on the issue, its various causes, the expanding reach of violence, and potential actions to combat what the UN News Centre refers to as "a plague that affects every country."

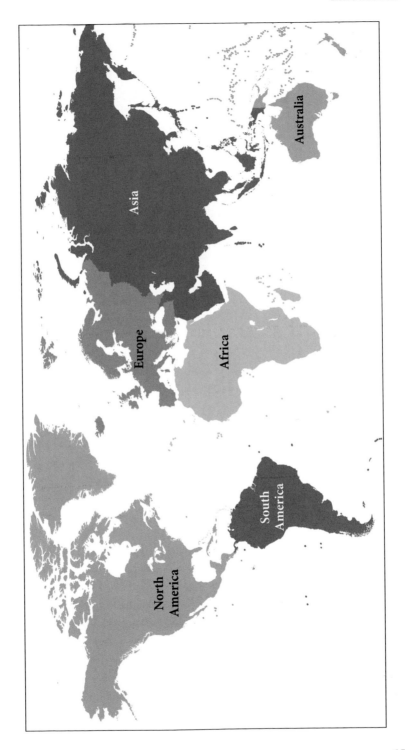

CHAPTER 1

What Constitutes Honor Killing?

The Difference Between Honor Killing and Domestic Violence

Phyllis Chesler

In the following viewpoint, Phyllis Chesler, cofounder of the Association for Women in Psychology and the National Women's Health Network, argues that honor killing is a unique form of murder. In contrast to some feminist groups, Chesler insists that honor killing is not at all the same as Western-style domestic violence or femicide, the killing of women. Chesler, who is a former professor of psychology and women's studies, maintains that the incidence of honor killing is on the rise and that closely related family members continue to inflict their brand of justice on girls and women.

As you read, consider the following questions:

1. Is honor killing escalating? According to Chesler, what might be a cause?
2. What are the two types of honor killing, and what is the significance of each type?
3. In the article, what does it mean to be "Westernized"?

To combat the epidemic of honor killings requires understanding what makes these murders unique. They differ from plain and psychopathic homicides, serial killings, crimes of passion, revenge killings, and domestic violence. Their motivation is different and

"Worldwide Trends in Honor Killings," by Phyllis Chesler, *Middle East Quarterly*, Spring 2010, pp. 3-11. (http://www.meforum.org/2646/worldwide-trends-in-honor-killings). Reprinted by permission.

based on codes of morality and behavior that typify some cultures, often reinforced by fundamentalist religious dictates. In 2000, the United Nations estimated that there are 5,000 honor killings every year.[1] That number might be reasonable for Pakistan alone, but worldwide the numbers are much greater. In 2002 and again in 2004, the U.N. brought a resolution to end honor killings and other honor-related crimes. In 2004, at a meeting in The Hague about the rising tide of honor killings in Europe, law enforcement officers from the U.K. announced plans to begin reopening old cases to see if certain murders were, indeed, honor murders.[2] The number of honor killings is routinely underestimated, and most estimates are little more than guesses that vary widely. Definitive or reliable worldwide estimates of honor killing incidence do not exist.

Most honor killings are not classified as such, are rarely prosecuted, or when prosecuted in the Muslim world, result in relatively light sentences.[3] When an honor killing occurs in the West, many people, including the police, still shy away from calling it an honor killing. In the West, both Islamist and feminist groups, including domestic violence activists, continue to insist that honor killings are a form of Western-style domestic violence or femicide (killing of women).[4] They are not.[5] This study documents that there are at least two types of honor killings and two victim populations. Both types differ significantly from each other, just as they differ from Western domestic femicide. One group has an average age of seventeen; the other group's average age is thirty-six. The age difference is a statistically significant one.

Families Killing Their Young Women

The study's findings indicate that honor killings accelerated significantly in a 20-year period between 1989 and 2009.[6] This may mean that honor killings are genuinely escalating, perhaps as a function of jihadist extremism and Islamic fundamentalism, or that honor killings are being more accurately reported and prosecuted, especially in the West, but also in the East. The expansion of the Internet may account for wider reporting of these incidents.

The worldwide average age of victims for the entire population is twenty-three. This is true for all geographical regions. Thus, wherever an honor killing is committed, it is primarily a crime against young people. Just over half of these victims were daughters and sisters; about a quarter were wives and girlfriends of the perpetrators. The remainder included mothers, aunts, nieces, cousins, uncles, or non-relatives.

Honor killings are a family collaboration. Worldwide, two-thirds of the victims were killed by their families of origin. Murder by the family of origin was at its highest (72 percent) in the Muslim world and at its lowest in North America (49 percent); European families of origin were involved almost as often as those in the Muslim world, possibly because so many are first- or second-generation immigrants and, therefore, still tightly bound to their native cultures. Alternatively, this might be due to the Islamist radicalization of third or even fourth generations. Internationally, fathers played an active role in over one-third of the honor murders. Fathers were most involved in North America (52 percent) and least involved in the Muslim world; in Europe, fathers were involved in more than one-third of the murders.

Worldwide, 42 percent of these murders were carried out by multiple perpetrators, a characteristic which distinguishes them considerably from Western domestic femicide. A small number of the murders worldwide involved more than one victim. Multiple murders were at their highest in North America and at their lowest in Europe. In the Muslim world, just under a quarter of the murders involved more than one victim. Additional victims included the dead woman's children, boyfriend, fiancé, husband, sister, brother, or parents.

Worldwide, more than half the victims were tortured; i.e., they did not die instantly but in agony. In North America, over one-third of the victims were tortured; in Europe, two-thirds were tortured; in the Muslim world, half were tortured. Torturous deaths include: being raped or gang-raped before being killed; being strangled or bludgeoned to death; being stabbed many times (10 to 40 times);

being stoned or burned to death; being beheaded, or having one's throat slashed.

Finally, worldwide, 58 percent of the victims were murdered for being "too Western" and/or for resisting or disobeying cultural and religious expectations. The accusation of being "too Western" was the exact language used by the perpetrator or perpetrators. Being "too Western" meant being seen as too independent, not subservient enough, refusing to wear varieties of Islamic clothing (including forms of the veil), wanting an advanced education and a career, having non-Muslim (or non-Sikh or non-Hindu) friends or boyfriends, refusing to marry one's first cousin, wanting to choose one's own husband, choosing a socially "inferior" or non-Muslim (or non-Sikh or non-Hindu) husband; or leaving an abusive husband. There were statistically significant regional differences for this motive. For example, in North America, 91 percent of victims were murdered for being "too Western" as compared to a smaller but still substantial number (71 percent) in Europe. In comparison, only 43 percent of victims were killed for this reason in the Muslim world.

Less than half (42 percent) of the victims worldwide were murdered for committing an alleged "sexual impropriety"; this refers to victims who had been raped, were allegedly having extramarital affairs, or who were viewed as "promiscuous" (even where this might not refer to actual sexual promiscuity or even sexual activity). However, in the Muslim world, 57 percent of victims were murdered for this motive as compared to 29 percent in Europe and a small number (9 percent) in North America.

What the Age Differences Mean

This study documents that there are at least two different kinds of honor killings and/or two different victim populations: one made up of female children and young women whose average age is seventeen, the other composed of women whose average age is thirty-six. Both kinds of honor murders differ from Western domestic femicide.

In the non-immigrant West, serious domestic violence exists which includes incest, child abuse, marital rape, marital battering, marital stalking, and marital post-battering femicide. However, there is no cultural pattern of fathers specifically targeting or murdering their teenage or young adult daughters, nor do families of origin participate in planning, perpetrating, justifying, and valorizing such murders. Clearly, these characteristics define the classic honor killing of younger women and girls.

The honor murders of older women might seem to resemble Western-style domestic femicide. The victim is an older married woman, usually a mother, who is often killed by her husband but also by multiple perpetrators (30 percent of the time). Worldwide, almost half (44 percent) of those who kill older-age victims include members of either the victim's family of origin or members of her husband's family of origin. This is extremely rare in a Western domestic femicide; the husband who kills his wife in the West is rarely assisted by members of his family of origin or by his in-laws.

However, in the Muslim world, older-age honor killing victims are murdered by their own families of origin nearly two-thirds of the time. This suggests that the old-world custom has changed somewhat in Europe where the victim's family of origin participates in her murder only one-third (31 percent) of the time. Thus far, in North America, no members of the family of origin have participated in the honor killing of an older-age victim. Whether North America will eventually come to resemble Europe or even the Muslim world remains to be seen, as this will be influenced by immigration and other demographic factors. Finally, nearly half the older-age victims are subjected to a torturous death. However, the torture rate was at its highest (68 percent) in Europe for female victims of all ages. The torture rate was 35 percent and 51 percent in North America and in the Muslim world, respectively.

Worldwide, younger-age victims were killed by their families of origin 81 percent of the time. In North America, 94 percent were killed by their family of origin; this figure was 77 percent in Europe and 82 percent in the Muslim world. In North America, fathers had a hands-on role in 100 percent of the cases when the daughter was eighteen-years-old or younger. Worldwide, younger-age women and girls were tortured 53 percent of the time; however, in Europe, they were tortured between 72 and 83 percent of the time—significantly more than older-age women worldwide.

Western Responses to Honor Killing

Many Western feminists and advocates for victims of domestic violence have confused Western domestic violence or domestic femicide (the two are different) with the honor killings of older-age victims. Representatives of Islamist pressure groups including Council on American-Islamic Relations (CAIR) and the Canadian Islamic Congress, various academics (e.g., Ajay Nair, Tom Keil), activists (e.g., Rana Husseini), and religious leaders (e.g., Abdulhai Patel of the Canadian Council of Imams) have insisted that honor killings either do not exist or have nothing to do with Islam; that they are cultural, tribal, pre-Islamic customs, and that, in any event, domestic violence exists everywhere.[7] Feminists who work with the victims of domestic violence have seen so much violence against women that they are uncomfortable singling out one group of perpetrators, especially an immigrant or Muslim group. However, Western domestic femicide differs significantly from honor killing.[8]

Former National Organization for Women (NOW) president Kim Gandy compared the battered and beheaded Aasiya Hassan[9] to the battered (but still living) pop star Rihanna and further questioned whether Hassan's murder was an honor killing:

> Is a Muslim man in Buffalo more likely to kill his wife than a Catholic man in Buffalo? A Jewish man in Buffalo? I don't know the answer to that, but I know that there is plenty of violence to go around—and that the long and sordid history of oppressing women in the name of religion surely includes Islam, but is not limited to Islam.[10]

At the time of the Hassan beheading, a coalition of domestic violence workers sent an (unpublished) letter to the Erie County district attorney's office and to some media stating that this was not an honor killing, that honor killings had nothing to do with Islam, and that sensationalizing Muslim domestic violence was not only racist but also served to render invisible the much larger incidence of both domestic violence and domestic femicide. They have a point, but they also miss the point, namely, that apples are not oranges and that honor killings are not the same as Western domestic femicides.

One might argue that the stated murder motive of being "too Westernized" may, in a sense, overlap substantively with the stated and unstated motives involved in Western domestic femicide. In both instances, the woman is expected to live with male violence and to remain silent about it. She is not supposed to leave—or to leave with the children or any other male "property." However, the need to keep a woman isolated, subordinate, fearful, and dependent through the use of violence does not reflect a Western cultural or religious value; rather, it reflects the individual, psychological pathology of the Western batterer-murderer. On the other hand, an honor killing reflects the culture's values aimed at regulating female behavior—values that the family, including the victim's family, is expected to enforce and uphold.

Further, such cultural, ethnic, or tribal values are not often condemned by the major religious and political leaders in developing Muslim countries or in immigrant communities in the West. On the contrary, such communities maintain an enforced silence on all matters of religious, cultural, or communal "sensitivity." Today, such leaders (and their many followers) often tempt, shame, or force Muslim girls and women into wearing a variety of body coverings including the *hijab* (head covering), *burqa*, or *chadari* (full-body covering) as an expression of religiosity and cultural pride or as an expression of symbolic resistance to the non-Muslim West.[11] Muslim men are allowed to dress like Westerners, and no one challenges the ubiquitous use of Western technology, including airplanes, cell phones, the Internet, or satellite television as un-Islamic. But Muslim women are expected to bear the burden of upholding these ancient and allegedly religious customs of gender apartheid.

It is clear that Muslim girls and women are murdered for honor in both the West and the East when they refuse to wear the *hijab* or choose to wear it improperly. In addition, they are killed for behaving in accepted Western or modern ways when they express a desire to attend college, have careers, live independent lives, have non-Muslim friends (including boyfriends with whom they may or may not be sexually involved), choose their own husbands, refuse to marry their first cousins, or want to leave an abusive husband. This "Westernization" trend also exists in Muslim countries but to a lesser extent. Allegations of unacceptable "Westernization" accounted for 44 percent of honor murders in the Muslim world as compared to 71 percent in Europe and 91 percent in North America.

Tempted by Western ideas, desiring to assimilate, and hoping to escape lives of subordination, those girls and women who exercise their option to be Western are killed—at early ages and in particularly gruesome ways. Frightening honor murders may constitute an object lesson to other Muslim girls and women about what may happen to them if they act on the temptation to do more than serve their fathers and brothers as domestic servants, marry their first cousin, and breed as many children as possible. The deaths of females already living in the West may also be intended as lessons for other female immigrants who are expected to lead subordinate and segregated lives amid the temptations and privileges of freedom. This is especially true in Europe where large Muslim ghettos have formed in the past few decades. It is particularly alarming to note that in Europe 96 percent of the honor killing perpetrators are Muslims.

The level of primal, sadistic, or barbaric savagery shown in honor killings towards a female family intimate more closely approximates some of the murders in the West perpetrated by serial killers against prostitutes or randomly selected women. It also suggests that gender separatism, the devaluation of girls and women, normalized child abuse, including arranged child marriages of both boys and girls, sexual repression, misogyny (sometimes inspired by misogynist interpretations of the Qur'an), and the demands made by an increase in the violent ideology of jihad all lead to murderous levels of aggression towards girls and women. One only has to kill a few girls and women to keep the others in line. Honor killings are, in a sense, a form of domestic terrorism, meant to ensure that Muslim women wear the Islamic veil, have Muslim babies, and mingle only with other Muslims.

Since Muslim immigration and, therefore, family networks are more restricted in North America than in Europe, honor-killing fathers may feel that the entire burden for upholding standards for female behavior falls heavily upon them and them alone. This may account for the fact that fathers are responsible 100 percent of the time for the honor murders of the youngest-age victims. In Europe and in the Muslim world, that burden may more easily be shared by sons and brothers, grandfathers, uncles, and male cousins.

What Must Be Done

How can this problem be addressed? Immigration, law enforcement, and religious authorities must all be included in education, prevention, and prosecution efforts in the matter of honor killings.

In addition, shelters for battered Muslim girls and women should be established and multilingual staff appropriately trained in the facts about honor killings. For example, young Muslim girls are frequently lured back home by their mothers. When a shelter resident receives such a phone call, the staff must immediately go on high alert. The equivalent of a federal witness protection program for the intended targets of honor killings should be created; England has already established such a program.[12] Extended safe surrogate family networks must be created to replace existing family networks; the intended victims themselves, with enormous assistance, may become each other's "sisters."

In addition, clear government warnings must be issued to Muslim, Sikh, and Hindu immigrants and citizens: Honor killings must be prosecuted in the West, and perpetrators, accomplices, and enablers must all be prosecuted. Participating families should be publicly shamed. Criminals must be deported after they have served their sentences.

Western judicial systems and governments have recently begun to address this problem. In 2006, a Danish court convicted nine members of a clan for the honor murder of Ghazala Khan.[13] In 2009, a German court sentenced a father to life in prison for having ordered his son to murder his sister for the family honor while the 20-year-old son was sentenced to nine and a half years.[14] In another case, a British court, with the help of testimony from the victim's mother and fiancé, convicted a father of a 10-year-old honor murder after the crime was reclassified;[15] and, for the first time, the Canadian government informed new immigrants:

> Canada's openness and generosity do not extend to barbaric cultural practices that tolerate spousal abuse, "honour killings," female genital mutilation or other gender-based violence. Those guilty of these crimes are severely punished under Canada's criminal laws.[16]

Islamic gender apartheid is a human rights violation and cannot be justified in the name of cultural relativism, tolerance, anti-racism, diversity, or political correctness. As long as Islamist groups continue to deny, minimize, or obfuscate the problem, and government and police officials accept their inaccurate versions of reality, women will continue to be killed for honor in the West.

The battle for women's rights is central to the battle for Europe and for Western values. It is a necessary part of true democracy, along with freedom of religion, tolerance for homosexuals, and freedom of dissent. Here, then, is exactly where the greatest battle of the twenty-first century is joined.

[...]

Methodology

This study analyzes 172 incidents and 230 honor-killing victims. The information was obtained from the English-language media around the world with one exception. There were 100 victims murdered for honor in the West, including 33 in North America and 67 in Europe. There were 130 additional victims in the Muslim world. Most of the perpetrators were Muslims, as were their victims, and most of the victims were women.

The perpetrators and victims in this study lived in the following twenty-nine countries or territories: Afghanistan, Albania, Bangladesh, Belgium, Canada, Denmark, Egypt, France, Gaza Strip, Germany, India, Iran, Iraq, Israel, Italy, Jordan, Netherlands, Norway, Pakistan, Russia, Saudi Arabia, Scotland, Sweden, Switzerland, Syria, Turkey, United Kingdom, United States, and the West Bank.

In general, statistically significant interactions were found for age, geographical region, the participation of multiple perpetrators (mainly members of the victim's family of origin, including the victim's father), family position, multiple victims, the use of torture, and the stated motive for the murder. Between 1989 and 2009, honor killings also escalated over time in a statistically significant way.

Worldwide, the majority of victims were women; a mere 7 percent were men. Only five men were killed by their families of origin whereas the rest of the male victims were killed by the families of the women with whom they were allegedly consorting or planning to consort with either within or outside of marriage. The murdered male victims were usually perceived as men who were unacceptable due to lower class or caste status, because the marriage had not been arranged by the woman's family of origin, because they were not the woman's first cousin, or because the men allegedly engaged in pre- or extramarital sex. Men were rarely killed when they were alone; 81 percent were killed when the couple in question was together.

Although Sikhs and Hindus do sometimes commit such murders, honor killings, both worldwide and in the West, are mainly Muslim-on-Muslim crimes. In this study, worldwide, 91 percent of perpetrators were Muslims. In North America, most killers (84 percent) were Muslims, with only a few Sikhs and even

---

Can the Murder of Women and Girls Be Stopped?

Each week brings horrific new headlines stating that, somewhere around the world, a woman or girl has been killed by a male relative for allegedly bringing dishonor upon her family. According to the U.N. High Commissioner for Human Rights, "In the name of preserving family 'honor,' women and girls are shot, stoned, burned, buried alive, strangled, smothered and knifed to death with horrifying regularity." Between 5,000 and 20,000 so-called honor killings are committed each year, based on long-held beliefs that any female who commits—or is suspected of committing—an "immoral" act should be killed to "restore honor" to her family. Honor killings are deeply rooted in ancient patriarchal and fundamentalist traditions, which some judicial systems legitimize by pardoning offenders or handing out light sentences. Human-rights organizations are demanding that governments and the international community act more forcefully to stop honor killings, but officials in some countries are doing little to protect women and girls within their borders.

- "Honor Killings: Can Murders of Women and Girls Be Stopped?" by Robert Kiener,
SAGE Publications, April 19, 2011.

---

fewer Hindus perpetrating honor killings; in Europe, Muslims comprised an even larger majority at 96 percent while Sikhs were a tiny percentage. In Muslim countries, obviously almost all the perpetrators were Muslims. With only two exceptions, the victims were all members of the same religious group as their murderers.

In the West, 76 individuals or groups of multiple perpetrators killed one hundred people. Of these perpetrators, 37 percent came from Pakistan; 17 percent were of Iraqi origin while Turks and Afghans made up 12 and 11 percent, respectively. The remainder, just under a quarter in all, came from Albania, Algeria, Bosnia, Egypt, Ethiopia, Guyana, India, Iran, Morocco, and the West Bank.

Footnotes

1. "Ending Violence against Women and Girls," *State of the World Population 2000* (New York: United Nations Population Fund, 2000), chap. 3.
2. *BBC News*, June 22, 2004.

3. Yotam Feldner, "'Honor' Murders–Why the *Perps* Get off Easy,» *Middle East Quarterly,* Dec. 2000, pp. 41-50.

4. See, for example, *SoundVision.com*, Islamic information and products site, Aug. 24, 2000; Sheila Musaji, "The Death of Aqsa Parvez Should Be an Interfaith Call to Action," *The American Muslim*, Dec. 14, 2007; Mohammed Elmasry, Canadian Islamic Congress, *Fox News.com*, Dec. 12, 2007; Mustafaa Carroll, Dallas branch of the Council of American-Islamic Relations, *FoxNews.com*, Oct. 14, 2008.

5. Phyllis Chesler, "Are Honor Killings Simply Domestic Violence?" *Middle East Quarterly,* Spring 2009, pp. 61-9.

4. Canadian Islamic Congress, *Fox News.com*, Dec. 12, 2007; Mustafaa Carroll, Dallas branch of the Council of American-Islamic Relations, *FoxNews.com*, Oct. 14, 2008.

5. Phyllis Chesler, "Are Honor Killings Simply Domestic Violence?" *Middle East Quarterly,* Spring 2009, pp. 61-9.

6. According to the Pearson product-moment correlation coefficient, the most widely used measure of correlation or association.

7. See, for example, *SoundVision.com*, Aug. 24, 2000; Musaji, "The Death of Aqsa Parvez Should Be an Interfaith Call to Action"; Elmasry, *Fox News.com*, Dec. 12, 2007; Carroll, *FoxNews.com*, Oct. 14, 2008.

8. *Chesler*," Are Honor Killings Simply Domestic Violence?"; "A Civilized Dialogue about Islam and Honor Killing: When Feminist Heroes Disagree," *Chesler Chronicles*, Mar. 2, 2009; "Jordanian Journalist Rana Husseini on 'Murder in the Name of Honor: The True Story of One Woman's Heroic Fight Against an Unbelievable Crime,'" *Democracy Now*, Oct. 21, 2009.

9. *Fox News*, Feb. 16, 2009.

10. *Kim Gandy, NOW president,* "Below the Belt. No Woman, No Culture Immune to Violence against Women," Feb. 20, 2009.

11. *BBC News,* Oct. 5, 2006; Aisha Stacey, "Why Muslim Women Wear the Veil," IslamReligion.com, Nov 15, 2009.

12. James Brandon and Salam Hafez, *Crimes of the Community: Honour-based Violence in the UK* (London: Centre for Social Cohesion, 2008), pp. 136-40.

13. *Brussels Journal*, July 2, 2006.

14. *Deutsche Welle* (Bonn), Dec. 29, 2009.

15. *The Guardian* (London), Dec. 17, 2009.

16. *The National Post* (Don Mills, Ont.), Nov. 12, 2009.

Pandemic Violence Against Women Costs Society

Deutsche Gesellschaft für Technische Zusammenarbeit (GTZ)

In the following viewpoint, GTZ, which promotes gender equality and women's rights, hypothesizes that violence against women not only is a violation of basic human rights, but takes a tremendous toll in social and economic ways across the society in which it occurs. Comprising many forms, it is a multifaceted problem caused by interconnected institutional, social, and cultural causes. GTZ's Programme for Promoting Gender Equality and Women's Rights, based in Germany, specializes in international cooperation aimed at sustainable development opportunities.

As you read, consider the following questions:

1. According to the GTZ, in what forms does violence against women appear in societies?
2. What societal costs result from violence against women, per the authors?
3. What types of discrimination does GTZ think promotes violence against women?

International Framework and Definition

Violence against women is no longer regarded as a private matter, but as a serious violation of human rights. This is the result of the 1994 International Conference on Population and Development as well as the 1995 Fourth World Conference on Women. Moreover, a 1994 mandate established a Special Rapporteur on Violence against Women.

The United Nations defines violence against women in the Declaration on the Elimination of Violence against Women as *"any act of gender-based violence that results in, or is likely to result in, physical, sexual or psychological harm or suffering to women, including threats of such acts, coercion or arbitrary deprivation of liberty, whether occurring in public or in private life"* (United Nations 1993).

Forms and Facets of Violence Against Women

There are many forms of violence against women, including sexual, physical, or emotional abuse by intimate partners, family members or others; sexual harassment and abuse by authorities such as teachers, police officers or employers; trafficking for forced labour or sex; and traditional practices such as female genital mutilation, or forced or child marriages. Violence against women often ends with fatalities, such as in the case of honour killings. Systematic sexual abuse during conflict situations is another pervasive form of violence against women.

Violence against women happens in both the private and in the public sphere. It is a widespread and multi-faceted problem with a variety of persons in the roles of perpetrators and victims. However, to combat the phenomenon, other relevant factors such as health and education must be considered, as well as involving other actors such as police personnel, social workers and educators as well as politicians and legal authorities.

Magnitude and Costs of the Problem

Violence against women and girls is a problem of pandemic proportions. Worldwide, an estimated one in five women will be a victim of rape or attempted rape in her lifetime. One in three will have been beaten, coerced into sex or otherwise abused, usually by a family member or an acquaintance. The perpetrators—more often than not—go unpunished. Each year, hundreds of thousands of women and children are trafficked and enslaved; millions more are subjected to harmful practices such as female genital mutilation. Violence kills and disables as many women between the ages of 15 and 44 as cancer does. And its toll on women's health surpasses that of traffic accidents and malaria combined (See UNFPA 2005).

The social and economic costs of violence against women are enormous and have significant ripple effects throughout society. Violence against women not only causes suffering and poor health for those directly involved through individual effects such as an inability to work, loss of wages, and lessened ability to care for themselves and their children. But it also leads to major financial strains on all of society with regard to medical care, the judicial system, social services, social insurances, and unemployment, as well as productivity losses. The ILO estimates losses from stress and violence at work consume between 1 to 3.5 per cent of the gross domestic product (ILO 2001). Hence, the existence of violence against women remains a significant obstacle to reducing poverty, achieving gender equality and meeting the Millennium Development Goals (MDG).

Factors that Perpetuate Violence Against Women

There is no one single factor to account for violence against women. Several complex and interconnected institutional, social and cultural factors have kept women particularly vulnerable to the violence directed at them. In many countries women are discriminated against culturally, economically, legally and politically. These discriminations promote an environment in which women are subjected to violence.

Successful Approaches to Combat Violence Against Women

Research has shown that preventive interventions to stop violence against women cost less than financing the costs that result from violence against women. The 1994 Violence Against Women Act, for example, "resulted in an estimated net benefit of $16.4 billion" (WHO 2004). Considering the various factors responsible for violence against women, strategies and interventions should be designed within a comprehensive and integrated framework. The German Development Cooperation supports approaches to combat violence perpetrated against women in the fields of prevention and lobbying for improved legal frameworks as well as the training of relevant actors and networking as illustrated in the following examples.

Enhancing Women's Rights in Cambodia

Domestic violence is a widespread problem in Cambodia, which has weak prosecution rates because victims rarely bring their cases to court. The Ministry of Women's Affairs (MOWA) implemented a law that focuses on protection against violence. Beyond the improvement of the legal situation of women, this process changed the general attitude towards domestic violence. To accomplish this change of attitude, MOWA also worked with men. By offering services such as refuges and legal advice for battered women, the situation for victims of violence was improved.

Raising Awareness Through a Music Video on Violence Against Women in India

In cooperation with popular Indian singers, the non-governmental organisation "Breakthrough" developed a song and music clips as part of a multimedia campaign. The song "Mann ke Manjeeré," dealing with HIV and violence against women, reached more than 26 million households and triggered a broad public debate on the issue. It was on top of the MTV Charts for five months. In addition, it won the 2001 Indian Screen Award and was nominated as the best Indipop music video for the MTV Award.

Literature and links

GTZ: *www.gtz.de/gender*

GTZ has developed an exhibit on gender-based violence, which can be ordered as a travelling exhibit.

GTZ: *Ending violence against women and girls. 2005.*

ILO: *The cost of violence/stress at work and the benefits of a violence/stress-free working environment. 2001.*

UN: *In-depths study on all forms of violence against women: Report of the Secretary General. 2006.*

UNFPA 2005: *State of the world population 2005* and its multimedia exhibition at: *www.unfpa.org/endingviolence/home.html*

UNICEF: *Domestic violence against women and girls. 2000.* WHO: *The economic costs of interpersonal violence. 2004.*

UNIFEM: *www.unifem.org* and its Global Platform for Advocacy and Action: *www.unifem.org/campaigns/vaw*

Honor Killing Is an Extreme Form of Intimate Partner Violence

Janet I. Sigal

In the following viewpoint, Janet I. Sigal argues that honor killing is an extreme example of intimate partner violence, which occurs in certain circumstances when women are accused of behavior that is believed to bring a negative impact upon their families. She further states that it is often underreported and consequently the statistical number of murders is inaccurate. Sigal, a UN/NGO representative for the American Psychological Association, offers a multistep approach to alleviate gender-based violence.

As you read, consider the following questions:

1. According to the author, what is the most common form of violence against women?
2. What are the personal costs women suffer when affected by intimate partner violence?
3. How can domestic violence be stopped and what solutions must be used, according to Sigal?

D omestic violence is a pervasive problem worldwide that is of great concern to diplomats and NGO personnel at the UN. Leaders at the UN characterize domestic violence, also called intimate partner violence (IPV), as a violation of human rights for millions of women globally. These leaders, including former UN Secretary General Kofi Annan, support research which has identified the causes of IPV as patriarchal inequality between men and women which results in power and economic differentials (Haj-yahia, 2002). This inequality includes cultural norms which discriminate against women and condone violence by male perpetrators.

Gender-based violence adversely affects the UN's ability to successfully meet its MDGs, for example, MDG # 3, which relates to promoting equality and empowering women, and MDG # 5, which involves improving maternal health. Despite the efforts of the UN and the World Health Organization (WHO), programs to reduce or eliminate domestic violence have not been very effective.

Some Definitions

Domestic violence is defined as physical, psychological, or sexual violence occurring among family members.

Intimate Partner Violence (IPV) occurs between partners who are in marriages, cohabiting relationships, or while dating. The various forms of IPV include violent acts which cause physical, sexual, or psychological harm; economic control; and behavioral restrictions.

Honor crimes or honor killings occur within families or between intimate partners. Honor killings are the most extreme form of IPV in which mostly women are killed for alleged transgressions which negatively affect the "honor" of the family. These transgressions include being a rape victim, alleged adultery, or even speaking to a man who is not a relative. For example, recently, a father in Yemen burned his daughter to death after discovering that she had spoken with her fiancé on a cell phone before they were married. In another horrific example, in India, in 2012, a 14 year old girl who had been in an arranged marriage, returned to her family complaining of being tortured by her in-laws. A few days later she disappeared. Her brother found her living with an ex-boyfriend. The brother dragged her into the street, cut off her head, and walked to the police station to surrender while carrying her head. The family was "very proud" of the brother's actions because she had to be punished in order to restore the family's honor.

Some Statistics

IPV is the most common form of violence against women but also is one of the most under-reported crimes (Domestic Violence Statistics, 2014). For example, in Australia, Canada, Israel, South Africa, and the U.S., IPV accounts for between 40% and 70% of murdered women (Domestic Violence Statistics). However, because of under-reporting, these data are likely to be inaccurate.

Though widely understood as an underestimation, honor killings are estimated to be about 5,000 murders of women per year worldwide, with reports of approximately 950 honor killings yearly in Pakistan alone (UN News Service, 2010). Often, honor killings receive little or no punishment. In some cultures, the perpetrators simply apologize and are not given prison sentences if the apology is accepted.

Some Consequences

The Centers for Disease Control and Prevention (CDC) and the World Health Organization (WHO) have identified several different consequences of IPV for women (CDC, 2014; WHO, 2014):

- Physical consequences include the following:
- Mild to severe physical injury (e.g., broken bones, burns)
- Reproductive difficulties (e.g., miscarriages, excessive bleeding). Young girls are at high risk for this consequence. Girls who are forced into an arranged marriage to an older man and obligated to engage in sexual activity may not have a fully developed reproductive system.

Psychological consequences include the following:

- Depression

- Anxiety
- Post-Traumatic Stress Disorder (PTSD)
- Low self-esteem
- Fear of intimacy

Health consequences include the following:

- Chronic stress-related disorders (e.g., high blood pressure)
- HIV/AIDS and sexually transmitted diseases
- Suicide attempts and ideation
- Sleep disturbances
- Substance abuse/alcoholism
- Risky sexual behaviors
- Smoking

Intervention Programs

Mr. Ban Ki-moon, the current UN Secretary General, made the following statement regarding domestic violence, "Break the silence. When you witness violence against women and girls, do not sit back. Act" (UN Women, n.d.). Psychologists have offered explanations for IPV and have developed interventions designed to reduce this violent behavior. Within its cultural context, violent behavior is so complex and its specific cultural factors are so significant, that multi-factor and culturally sensitive interventions must be developed. Solutions to this gender-based violence problem must focus on the following:

1. *Legal and international agreements.* Laws must be passed and international agreements must be enforced to punish perpetrators. Leaders of countries that do not abide by international agreements and laws must be held accountable.

2. *Training for the police force, judiciary, and medical/mental health personnel.* These professions are typically male

dominated in many countries. Consequently, men are in a power position to ignore or minimize charges of IPV, while concurrently being "responsible for" adjudicating perpetrators and protecting and treating victims. These professions need training to ensure sensitivity to survivors and to take seriously accounts of abuse. For example, a student from India said that IPV victims are reluctant to report abuse because of fear that the police will laugh at them and send them back to the abusers.

3. *Academic education.* Education is important for empowering women and girls and for reducing IPV and domestic violence in the long term. Girls and women who are educated may be less vulnerable to abuse in relationships because they have acquired some skills for economic independence and might perceive that they have options, other than remaining within the relationship.

4. *Life skills training.* Children can be trained in early grades to use conflict resolution and other non-violent life skills.

5. *Change cultural attitudes and norms.* Changing attitudes and norms that condone, and even mandate, violence against women must occur. Social psychologists have informed us that information campaigns alone (e.g., cognitive awareness) will not change cultural attitudes, which are endemic in the society. The emotional aspects of "attitude," along with cognitive ones, must be used. Over time, attitude change results in new cultural norms.

6. *Involve boys and men in the change process.* In order for attitudes and norms to change, men and boys need to be involved in the efforts. Males typically listen to other males. Male-led conversations and interventions should stress IPV as a *human* problem, and not one just relevant to women.

7. *Increase safe havens.* There should be safe havens for women and girls to recuperate and receive medical and mental health treatment. The locations of these havens should be

confidential in order to avoid destruction and intimidation by perpetrators or other males.

8. *Use evidence-based psychotherapy when culturally appropriate.* In some cultures, cognitive behavioral therapy (CBT), an evidence-based therapy, has been used successfully to treat IPV survivors.

9. *Develop appropriate and culture-specific treatment/ intervention programs for perpetrators.* Globally, the traditional focus of treatment and intervention is on survivors, usually girls and women, but there should be parallel treatment/intervention programs for abusers. For example, Day, Chung, O'Leary, and Carson (2009) found that assessing for the *types* of batterers in mandated treatment programs is effective in determining the best therapy/intervention modality to motivate the perpetrator to change behavior. Intervention models that are chosen should be culturally relevant.

10. *Increase public awareness.* Involve the local and/or global media in increasing awareness about IPV and attitude change programs in order to eventually influence cultural norms. For instance, the Nigerian government was forced to attend to the horrific kidnapping of the nearly 300 girls from their school in Chibok earlier this year because of the international pressure to rescue them (i.e., *#Bring Back Our Girls*).

References

Centers for Disease Control and Prevention. (2014). Retrieved from http://www.cdc.gov/

Day, A., Chung, D., O'Leary, P., & Carson, E. (2009). Programs for men who perpetrate domestic violence: An examination of the issues underlying the effectiveness of intervention programs. *Journal of Family Violence, 24*(3), 203-212. DOI: 10.1007/s10896-008-9221-4.

Domestic violence statistics. (2014). Retrieved from http://

domesticviolencestatistics.org/ Haj-yahia, M.M. (2002). Beliefs of Jordanian women about wife beating. *Psychology of Women Quarterly, 26,* 282-291.

UN News Service. (2010). Impunity for domestic violence "Honour killings cannot continue"—U.N. Official. Retrieved from: http://www.un.org/apps/news/printnews.AR.asp?nid=33971

UN Women. (n.d.). Unite to end violence against women. Retrieved from: http://www.un.org/en/women/endviolence/situation.shtml

World Health Organization. (2014). Retrieved from http://www.who.int/en/

In Turkey, Headscarves and Honor Killings Are Inextricably Linked

Hulya Arik

In this viewpoint, Hulya Arik, at the time a PhD student in Geography at Canada's York University, explores the connection between the Islamic custom of veiling and honor-based violence. Arik argues that headscarves, though not always a tool of male oppression, have politicized Turkish women's bodies since the 1960s and created a culture wherein violence against women flourishes.

As you read, consider the following questions:

1. What does the author mean by "the Islamization of public space"?
2. How is honor killing defined in the Turkish context?
3. Will banning headscarves stop honor-based violence?

Introduction

In recent years, Turkish media has been occupied with rape trials in which final judgments are made in function of the victim's "lifestyle" and the woman's "honour." But beyond these cases, misogynous murders based on the male partner's jealousy or rage have always been part of the news landscape. In 2011, Human Rights Watch (HRW) reported that domestic and family-based violence on women are notoriously high in Turkey. According to

"Speaking of Women? Exploring Violence against Women through Political Discourses: A Case Study of Headscarf Debates in Turkey," by Hulya Arik, E-cadernos CES, vol. 16, June 1. 2012. http://eces.revues.org/1009. Licensed under CC BY 4.0 International.

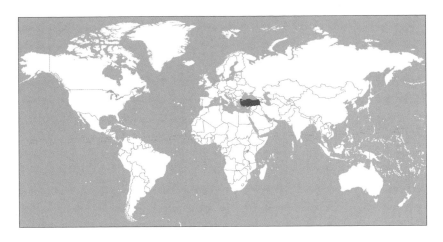

HRW, 42 per cent of women aged 15-60 in urban areas and 47 per cent of women in rural areas had experienced physical or sexual violence by their husbands or partners at some point in their lives (HRW, 2011). The Turkish Statistical Institute's figures show that, in the past five years, there has been a 30 per cent increase in the number of cases of rape and sexual harassment against women (TUIK, 2012). The HWR report also argues that there are too many gaps in the law and that authorities' infrequently enforce preventive and punitive measures (HRW, 2011).

Other than feminist groups and NGOs, no authority has publicized these figures or taken action to fix the problems they point to. Instead, the political scene has focused on women's need to regulate their behaviour and dress in public space in order to not get assaulted. For example, in February 2011, theology professor Orhan Ceker publicly stated, "Wearing décolleté is asking for rape" (Dekolte giyene, 2011). And in 2012, in the midst of a debate on the introduction of an abortion ban, the mayor of Ankara publicly stated that pregnancies as a result of rape should not be exempt from an abortion ban, since "it is the fault of the mother not the child who has to suffer" (Cocugun ne sucu, 2012). These statements support a gender regime in which female sexuality, as it is defined on and through the female body, becomes the measure of women's honour. The adoption, at a political level, of a patriarchal discourse with normative understandings of female honour justifies and reproduces the enactment of physical and sexual violence on women.

These public and political entanglements with women's dress, bodily rights and sexualities are not new in Turkey. Since 1923, when the Turkish Republic was created, there have been political traditions that have made women's bodies and sexualities into legitimate points of discussion. The secularist state has incorporated the modernly dressed Turkish woman into its political ideology and discourse, while political Islam, especially since the 1970s, has incorporated the headscarved woman into its political discourse. Since then, the headscarf has been persistently categorized as an issue of Islamist identity politics, rather than as a women's issue that pertains to women's sexuality.

Perceived as proof of the Islamization of public space, headscarved women have been stigmatized and become subject to bans and regulations since the early 1980s. Beyond being the symbol of Islamist politics and lifestyle, the headscarf became the embodiment of the conflict between the competing sexual regimes prescribed by Western forms of secularism and Islamist discourses in Turkey. Contained within the dichotomist framework of "modern, liberated Republican woman" and "religious headscarved woman," headscarf debates have formed a significant part of the political rivalries between political Islam and the defenders of the secularist state ideology. These discourses are masculinist not only in the sense that they prescribe and reproduce traditional gender roles for women, but also, in that they rely on constructions of female sexuality and honour that approve of and aggravate violence against women.

In this paper, I focus on the headscarf debates as an issue that has extensively occupied the Turkish political scene in the past three decades. I aim to show how wearing a headscarf, a practice quintessentially linked to female sexuality and honour, has been constructed as a political matter in ways that enable violence against women. Here, I perceive women's dress as a way of conveying and performing female sexuality and honour on the body (Werbner, 2007); and I discuss wearing a headscarf as a particular dress code. I take adoption of the headscarf as a way of ensuring women's sexuality and honour in public space (El Guindi, 1999; Werbner, 2007) which can be forced upon or taken up voluntarily, or neither of these, as any other form of dress can be. I introduce female honour into this debate as a fundamental aspect of the construction of a "proper" and "acceptable" form of femininity that significantly relies on female sexuality and chastity. Honour, specifically within the context of Turkey and the Middle Eastern societies in general, is constituted as the primary factor in enactment of violence against women. Through this, I demonstrate how debating the propriety and sincerity of the headscarf enables violence as it is actually a debate on women's bodies, sexualities and the construction of female honour.

By headscarf debates I refer to the political engagements with the headscarf bans, which, since the early 1980s have prohibited women from wearing headscarves at university campuses, state offices such as court rooms and the parliament, in addition to barring their employment by the state. These debates have involved political parties' reactions to the attempts for removal of the ban, discussing either women should wear headscarves or not, and how they should wear it in case they are allowed and where. These discussions have placed women's bodies and their sexualities at the centre of an ideological conflict, and solidified the tensions between the sexual regimes prescribed by republican secularism and by Islamism, as well as the moral claims each ideology can make over women's bodies. Formed within the discursive framework of patriarchy, headscarf debates have increased the discursive and physical tangibility of women's bodies and sexualities, and they have contributed to the gender regime that enables and tolerates violence against women.

In order to demonstrate this, firstly, I will provide an overview of Turkish modernization and secularism, with an emphasis on the construction of gender identities since the early Republican era. Secondly, I will briefly explain the emergence of the Islamic middle- and upper-classes and the parliamentary gains made by Islamist political parties since the 1970s. Through a survey of the trajectory of headscarf bans and debates in the 1980s, 1990s, and 2000s, I will show how women have been collapsed into a "headscarved" vs. "non-headscarved" dichotomy. I will examine, in particular, crises surrounding state protocols and receptions, as well as student reactions and court cases. I will then discuss the semantic field of sexuality, honour, and gendered violence in which the headscarf has been understood. And finally, to demonstrate the connection between headscarf, honour and violence, I will provide examples from national news media and social media, and artistic reflections on the issue to show how critiques of women's sexualities—such as sexually explicit remarks on headscarved and non-headscarved women—target women's bodies[1].

[...]

Semantics of the Headscarf

Studies on the meanings and cultural significance of the practice of wearing a headscarf, cross culturally and generally referred to as veiling, are inexorably rich. Various scholars of gender and Islam have studied and complicated the story of the "veil"[16] by introducing the culturally divergent and historical reasons for this practice (whether within religion or not) and by analysing in-depth religious texts. Fatima Mernissi is one of the first theoreticians of gender and Islam to offer a gender analysis of Quranic verses and the Hadiths (stories from Prophet Mohammed's life). According to her study, the veil, or hijab, was introduced and conceived in the Quran's Sura 33, as a means to regulate sexual relations within the community and to separate the private sphere of Prophet Mohammed and his wife Zaynab from public space and other men (Mernissi, 1991: 85). Fadwa El Guindi's (1999) study also suggests that the veil was used to regulate the Prophet's homestead, which was open to anyone at anytime for advice and counsel. In this sura, Mohammed was ordained to draw a curtain, a hijab, between his wives' privacy and the community (El Guindi, 1999: 153).

Besides segregating space and covering women's bodies, the hijab was also introduced as a solution to Mohammed's wives' problems in everyday life (Ahmed, 1986). Both Mernissi (1987) and El Guindi (1999) suggest that Mohammed's wives were the first women to adopt the Islamic practice of veiling to mark themselves as separate from "other women," who could be suspected of being slaves or prostitutes. Ayahs 30 and 31 of Sura 24 state that both men and women should control their gaze in public and not reveal their private (sexual) body parts and beauty. And in several other places in the Quran, women are directed to "draw their jilbab [a form of head covering] close round them [...] so that they may be recognized and not molested" (Quran 33:59 quoted in El Guindi, 1999: 154-155).

Mernissi's (1987, 1991) and El Guindi's (1999) analyses make it clear that the sexual segregation of spaces and the introduction of the hijab emerged from the need to regulate everyday life and sexual relations within the first Islamic community during the life of prophet Mohammed. However, El Guindi's (1999) cross-cultural and comparative analysis of the practice of veiling suggests that neither gender segregation nor women's veiling was specific to Islam at that time or to Arab societies. Also, Shirazi (2001) suggests that head covering was a common practice in pre-Islamic Iran as a marker of prestige and a symbol of status for upper-class women (also El Guindi, 1999: 16). Likewise, the practice of spatial segregation of women was established in Hellenic and Byzantine societies and was based on the lower status given to women (ibidem: 17). However, in Islam and Islamic societies, these practices became institutionalized through their incorporation into the Islamic texts (Ahmed, 1986).

As studies indicate, these practices are rooted in the regulation of sexualities through control of bodies and spaces. Mernissi puts it succinctly: "Muslim sexuality is territorial" (2003: 489). In her chapter "The Meaning of Spatial Boundaries," Mernissi contends that Muslim sexuality is regulated through a strict allocation of space to each sex and "an elaborate ritual for resolving the contradictions arising from the inevitable intersections of spaces" (Mernissi, 2003: 489). Having an important place in sexual spatial regulations, the concept of veiling gains significance in a three-dimensional perspective: visual, spatial, and ethical (Mernissi, 1991: 93). First, the veil visibly "hides" certain parts of a woman's body from public gaze; secondly, it spatially separates and marks a border between bodies who are considered illicit (because they exist outside of marriage or familial ties); and, thirdly, "it belongs to the realm of the forbidden" (Mernissi, 1991: 93).

This third aspect is crucial to the ways women's bodies are regulated according to Islamic discourses. In her book *Beyond the Veil* (1987) Mernissi argues that within Islamic discourse, the maintenance of social order depends on the spatial confinement of women's bodies. Because of her strong sexuality, the woman poses a threat to the harmony of the ummet (the Islamic community) (Rhouni, 2009: 166). In her critique, Rhouni (2009) suggests that Mernissi's take on the degraded status of women in Islamic societies is based on Islam's ready assumption of the power of female sexuality, which needs to remain under the control of men, who are considered mentally, physically, and morally superior. Although Mernissi's analysis has been critiqued for essentializing Islam and analysing it from a modernist perspective in isolation from wider cultural and patriarchal influences (see Ahmed, 1992, Rhouni, 2009), it raises points about Islam and sexuality that still pose challenges to current Islamic identities and discourses[17].

Islamic forms of gender segregation and veiling can be said to have emerged from already-existing forms of patriarchal relations and practices and been consolidated into an Islamic discourse. However, since there is no singular Islamic discourse, these practices have never shown a unitary and homogenous quality as is portrayed through Orientalist discourses. In their meanings and practice, gender segregation and veiling have shown considerable variety and inconsistency. As El Guindi argues, hijab, veil, burqu, jilbab, headscarf, and purdah have different meanings and connotations that deserve individual focus from a cross-cultural perspective (El Guindi, 1999). It is the Eurocentric perspective that subsumes all forms of veiling under the concept of "veil" or hijab and essentializes them as proof of women's oppression within a framework of "veil-harem-eunuchs-seclusion-polygamy" (El Guindi, 1999: 3-4).

It can be argued that the totalizing Orientalist view of Islamic societies has not only epitomized the image of oppressed woman, but has also imagined and reproduced an overtly sexualized and eroticized view. For instance, Mernissi (2001) explores the construction of the image of Muslim women in European literature and art as passive sexual objects in harems. Similarly, Yeğenoğlu (1998) investigates the representation of the veil and the Western fascination with veiled women due to their invisibility and inaccessibility to the Western gaze. She suggests that the "veil is one of those tropes through which Western fantasies of penetration into the mysteries of the Orient and access to the interiority of the other is achieved" (Yeğenoğlu, 2003: 543). In the same vein, Shirazi investigates the semantics of veiling by analysing the plentiful visual and printed material on the veil. By focusing on the role of the veil in popular culture, such as its use to advertise Western products, she explores how fixed sexual images of Middle Eastern women have been imagined in the Western mind, often ascribing an erotic meaning to the veil (2001: 11).

Veiling, however, cannot be considered only as a tool for the regulation of women's sexuality or as an eroticized construct in Orientalist discourses. It is also a practice that equips women, and communities, with tools to resist hegemonizing discourses and gendered power relations. Veiling has had a significant meaning in constructions of anti-colonialist movements and in the development of postcolonial nationalisms. Frantz Fanon's work (1965) on French colonialism and the Algerian nationalist liberation movement presents the veiled female body as a form of resistance to the modernizing and secularizing projects of

Western imperialism. Lila Abu-Lughod's early work (1986) on cultural constructions of gender and honour in a Bedouin society also presents examples of how women use veiling to position themselves within a patriarchal social order and how women empower themselves through meanings of sexuality and honour that are inherent to veiling. More recently, Saba Mahmood's (2005) work on the women's mosque movement in Egypt presents a compelling view of women's deliberate adoption of veiling and study of Islamic knowledge to gain power and authority in an area that has previously been reserved for males.

Whether textual analyses of Islamic discourse or examinations of totalizing Orientalist discourses, studies on veiling converge on one point: veiling's sexualizing aspects. As intended by the Quranic verses, as a concept for sexual spatial regulation, and as an aspect of women's dress, the veil has publicly marked the boundaries of sexual interaction in public space and on women's bodies. As Mernissi mentioned in her three-dimensional analyses, the veil connotes what is forbidden: a woman's sexual privacy. It is a practice that "underscores the sexual dimension of any interaction between men and women" (Mernissi, 2003: 491). If we put it another way, veiling is a practice that underscores what we consider to be female honour.

As I will describe in the next part, the concept of honour is intrinsically connected to the regulation of sexual space and behaviour, which in the case of Islamic discourse, becomes synonymous with the veil. Explanations that refer to Mohammed's life indicate that the veil was intended to secure women's privacy and "decency" in public space. European fantasies of unveiling the Oriental woman are symbolically connected to a desire to break the honour of women and, thus, to rupture the sexual social order that the community depends on. Even though they are effaced from today's public political discourses, moral crises related to the headscarf conflict in Turkey have emerged from the moral claims veiling makes through its regulation of female sexuality and honour. If the headscarf conflict in Turkey is a moral one, as I will argue, it is because of the veiling practice's regulation of sexuality and honour of women and the moral claims made through women's bodies.

Honour

In 2008, during the debate and controversy caused by JDP's proposal to amend the constitution to remove the headscarf ban at universities and in public employment, one of the prime minister's advisors, Cuneyt Zapsu, said, "Asking a woman to take off her headscarf is the same thing as asking a woman on the street to take off her panties." (Turbanini cikar, 2008) Out of all the controversial statements made during this debate, this was the most explicit reference to the sexualizing aspects of the headscarf and its significance for a woman's honour. More significantly, this statement underscored the potential of sexual violence that is inherent in the headscarf debates, a form of violence that cannot be dissociated from the construction of honour.

Studies on gender and honour, and the relationship between them in Turkey and surrounding geographies, almost unexceptionally look at their significance within the context of violence against women. As a concept so central to constructions of female sexuality in Turkey, honour subsumes all the cultural codes and meanings that enable and justify a violence that seeks to control women's bodies. As Sirman (2004) contends, the concept of honour pertains to both men and women, and it refers to one's ability to live up to the standards of femininity and masculinity. However, because of the asymmetries in the social construction of gender, a man's honour is measured by his ability to undertake his social responsibilities and to control his sexuality and that of the woman he is responsible for (Sirman, 2004: 44). On the other hand, a woman's honour is linked only to her sexuality, and it is defined within the private sphere in which she belongs (Akkoc, 2004). In this context, female honour becomes a key determinant in women's experiences, because social constructions of love and honour place women in a position that requires controlling their sexuality (being chaste) and demanding them to be sexually accountable to the family and even to the community (Sirman, 2004).

The most common phenomena through which honour and violence have been examined are honour crimes and domestic violence. Within the Turkish context, "honour crime," and more specifically "honour killing," is used as a "generic term to refer to the premeditated murder of a preadolescent, adolescent or adult women by one or more male members of the immediate family or the extended family" (Sev'er and Yurdakul, 2001: 964-965). Upon suspicion or proof of a victim's sexual impropriety, family members form a family council to decide on the woman's punishment—death in the case of honour killings (Sev'er and Yurdakul, 2001). However, even though various forms of sexual violence such as domestic violence, sexual harassment, and rape are also defined as honour crimes, they cannot be limited to the concept of honour alone. In her analysis of the social conditions that produce honour-related crimes and domestic violence, Sirman (2004: 39) refers to these crimes as an "infringement of women's human rights, including their right to work, to travel, to their own bodies, and finally their rights to life."

The problem with honour killings and the reason they persist is that they are considered "traditional" and thus perceived as doomed to disappear with the advancement of modernity, education, and progress (Sirman, 2004). However, as Sirman (2004) suggests, in postcolonial nation-states the notion of honour is reproduced in the new subject and is still based on "traditional" notions of femininity and female sexuality. The state supports the construction of gender identities through law, and since honour is considered a constitutive element in the making of society, honour crimes are perceived as an extension of the protection of virginity and gender values essential to the maintenance of the social order (2004).

In her study on forced virginity examinations in high schools in Turkey, Parla shows how the state defended these examinations as "a vital means of upholding 'our practices, customs, and traditions'" (Parla, 2001: 67). Until 2004, the Turkish penal code assigned reduced penalties to perpetuators of most honour-related crimes on the legal basis of "grievous unjust provocation," "which refers to a situation when a woman is suspected of bringing dishonour to her family as having provoked her murderers unjustly" (Sirman, 2004: 41). This gender bias is even more obvious in the categorization of attacks on the body as breaches of individual rights only when a male body is attacked (Parla, 2001: 77). As Parla (2001) puts it, attacks on the female body are considered an infringement, not of individual rights, but of the family order.

In judgements of sexual violence cases, discourses associating women's dress with her honour and agency have been prominent. Wolf (1997, cited in Entwistle 2000: 22) gives examples of rape cases in the United States, where (except in Florida) lawyers can legally cite the victim's dress at the time of the attack and whether or not the victim was "sexually attractive." The patriarchal discourse that is pervasive in the court system puts women in a position where they can be blamed for "asking for it" because of how they were dressed at the time of the attack (Entwistle, 2000; Moor, 2010). From this perspective, veiling in general, and the practice of wearing a headscarf specifically need to be considered in their efficacy in either "provoking" or "deterring" sexual assault or attacks. As Secor's (2002) research on migrant and working-class women in Istanbul also demonstrates, women use the headscarf to avoid harassment on the streets and to protect their honour in public.

By covering body parts that are considered as private and sexual, the practice of wearing a headscarf or veil embodies certain codes of honour, which, in most cases, become the criteria that determine the range of women's experiences—from being respected to being harassed. As demonstrated by research on Islamic texts, the initial intention of putting on a veil, or headscarf, conveys certain meanings on the female body, defines a "decent and honourable" female identity, and draws the boundary between public and private on the body of the female subject. Thus, contesting the propriety of such practice, as is the contestation of any form of female dress (such as the mini-skirt), puts women in a morally obscure space where their sexuality becomes questionable, thus open to violence.

From Headscarf Debates to Violence against Women: A Few Examples

When looking at the conflict between secularism and Islamism, it is important to acknowledge that both regimes and the practices they endorse (veiling/unveiling), operate by defining and debating female sexuality, honour, and privacy. During the past three decades, especially since political Islam started posing "threats" to the secular order, perceived discrepancies between these sexual regimes have become sharper and more visible. As Cinar points out (2008), the headscarf becomes a subversive force in the secular public sphere, because it asserts its own unconventional and non-secular (Islamic) norms of privacy and sexual modesty. Secularist norms, on the other hand, assert different public-private boundaries by specifically leaving the hair and neck, which are considered private aspects of female embodiment, open to public gaze (Cinar, 2008: 903).

Whenever the "issue of the headscarf" has been on the public agenda (whether in parliament, in public political discourse, in newspaper columns, or in the claims of various NGOs and feminist groups), its tension has become part of everyday life, too. As I observed from my surroundings and in the national news media, it became all too easy to pass judgement on a headscarved woman and to ask if she was sincere in her adoption of the headscarf or if she is using it just as a tool for Islamist politics. Thus, headscarved women became objects of attention and surveillance in terms of their congruence with the entirety of Islamic principles of sexual modesty.

A picture of a headscarved woman that has been circulated in emails and on social media in the past few years exemplifies this objectification. In this picture, there is a woman sitting on grass by a lake. She is wearing a black top, a black headscarf, and denim trousers. The photo, taken from behind, shows the backside of her belly, revealing her underwear at the waistline and a little part of her buttock cleavage. The important part of the picture is the caption: "She will burn in hell for 80 years if a single string of her hair shows, that's why she has to cover her hair. She is waiting for a new fetwa[18] to cover her ass!"

This kind of moral outrage against women's "inappropriate" dress is not an uncommon phenomenon. Joan Scott's work on headscarf conflicts in France provides an enlightening account of the "string affair" in which school girls whose thongs were visible at the waistline were sent home (2007). However, in the case of the headscarved woman whose G-string or thong is visible at the waistline, the critiques point at the inconsistency between the moral claims made by the headscarf and the woman's dress style, perceived as sexually provocative. The persistence of the headscarf and the right-to-wear question in political debates makes headscarved women open to public scrutiny and despise. Similarly, this makes headscarved women who drink alcohol or show sexual intimacy in public open to violent remarks in campaigns against the headscarf.

Moral judgements in defence of the non-headscarved women have also been important. For example, in 2008, at the height of the debates surrounding JDP's proposal to amend the constitution to remove the headscarf ban, the major Islamic-dress company Armine launched a new commercial campaign. In large billboards all over Istanbul, Armine showed a beautifully dressed headscarved model, under which we could read, "Dressing is beautiful" (Giyinmek güzeldir). This campaign immediately drew considerable attention and criticism. Several columnists (Arman, 2007; Capa, 2007) expressed their unease with the punch line, as it equated dressing only with wearing the headscarf and thus implied that non-headscarved women were naked or not dressed "properly". The commercial campaign functioned within a semantic field in which "non-headscarf" was equated with nakedness, a state that is intimately connected to a lack of morals and honour and that puts women in a place deserving of sexual objectification and harassment.

The stark contrast between the moral claims made by "secularists" and "Islamists" is also reflected in the work of artists who look at the female body and forms of symbolic violence perpetuated on the female body. Neriman Polat, a visual artist based in Istanbul, produces photography and collages on issues such as class- and gender-based social inequalities, the roles of women in society, and violence against women (Polat, 2012). In a group exhibition called "Collective Privacy," Polat displayed her work "The Hasema[19] Series." The exhibit sought to draw attention to the changing notions of "privacy" and "collectivity" in a society of surveillance. In their collective statement, the artists placed special emphasis on the notion of privacy that is often referenced through women's bodies (Utku, 2010).

In this exhibition, Neriman Polat's work on the hasema questions how conflicting notions of the privacy of women's bodies are being "collectivized." In one of the installation images, Polat juxtaposes body-length images of two models posing for the camera, with a beach in the background. One of the women is wearing a bikini and her head is cut and pasted from a headscarved hasema model. The other woman, standing next to her, is wearing a hasema, but without a headscarf, since the head is cut and pasted from the non-headscarved bikini model. By creating this provocative image, the artist draws attention to the ways the bans on headscarves, the debates on women's bodies, and women's sexual representations become "collectivized." The image of these two women portrays the contradictions that are inherent to the ideological conflicts, and it shows that women's bodies and sexualities are at the heart of headscarf debates.

Conclusion

Neither the modernly-dressed non-headscarved republican Turkish woman, nor the "Islamist" headscarved women are devoid of moral notions of femininity. Although they might seem contradictory, constructions of the Republican woman and of the headscarved woman are embedded in the same heterosexual matrix that ascribes women with traditional roles of femininity, sexual modesty, and honour. Starting as early as the 1960s, and becoming more persistent into the 1980s, headscarf debates in Turkey have put women's bodies and sexualities under public and political spotlight. Through the headscarf debates, each discourse's idealized image and sexual construction of women's bodies have been further polarized. These debates actively engaged female sexuality and honour, and thus made them matters of everyday discussion and banal aspects of the social dynamics of Turkish society. The increasing number of cases of domestic violence and honour crimes cannot be considered in isolation from the political discourses that reify codes of female sexuality and honour, even when no concrete or direct correlation can be made.

In her work on geographies of slavery and the black female body, Kathryn McKittrick says,

> The point of sale [of the black female body on the auction block] marks the scale of the body as "sellable", thus abstracting human complexities and particularities and discursively naturalizing multi-scalar ideologies that justify local, regional and national violence and enslavement. (2006: 79)

I likewise argue that a multilayered objectification and othering of women, as headscarved or not, is occurring. The discourses over the headscarf allow the emergence of spaces of violence where the female body can be acted upon in terms of its physical integrity, sexuality, and mobility. As demonstrated by the aforementioned cases, the discourse over the headscarf reinforces the control of female bodies through the social construction of female sexuality and honour. It constructs the female body as a scale, which is discussible and measurable, and makes violence possible.

Bibliografia
Abu-Lughod, Lila (1986), *Veiled Sentiments: Honor and Poetry in a Bedouin Society*. Berkeley; Los Angles: California University Press.

Ahmed, Leila (1986), "Women and the Advent of Islam," *Signs*, 11(4), 665–691. DOI : 10.1086/494271

Ahmed, Leila (1992), *Women and Gender in Islam: Historical Roots of a Modern Debate*. New Haven, CT: Yale University Press.

Akkoç, Nebahat (2004), "The Cultural Basis of Violence in the Name of Honour," *in* Shahrazad Mojab and Nahla Abdo (eds.), *Violence in the Name of Honour*. İstanbul: Bilgi Üniversitesi Press House, 113-126.

Aktas, C. (2006). *Türbanın Yeniden İcadı [Reinvention of the Turban]*. Istanbul: Kapı Yayınları.

Arat, Yesim (1998), "Feminists, Islamists, and Political Change in Turkey," *Political Psychology*, 19(1), 117-131. DOI : 10.1111/0162-895X.00095

Arman, Ayse (2007) "Türban güzel sen çirkin tartışması (2)" *Hurriyet Newspaper*, May 26. Accessed on March 1st 2013, at http://hurarsiv.hurriyet.com.tr/goster/haber.aspx?id=6586063.

Asad, Talal (2003), *Formations of the Secular: Christianity, Islam and Modernity*. California: Stanford University Press.

Capa, Ebru (2007), "Afişe olduk cümleten" *Hurriyet Newspaper*, May 20. Accessed on March 1st 2013, at http://hurarsiv.hurriyet.com.tr/goster/haber.aspx?id=6541960&yazarid=100.

Casanova, Jose (2006), "Rethinking Secularization: A Global Comparative Perspective," *The Hedgehog Review*, Spring/Summer 06, 7-22.

Cinar, Alev (2005), *Modernity, Islam and Secularism in Turkey: Bodies, Places and Time*. Minneapolis: University of Minnesota Press.

Cinar, Alev (2008), "Subversion and Subjugation in the Public Sphere: Secularism and the Islamic Headscarf," *Signs: Journal of Women in Culture & Society*, 33(4), 891-913.

Cindoglu, Dilek; Zencirci, Gizem (2008), "The Headscarf in Turkey in the Public and State Spheres," *Middle Eastern Studies*, 44(5), 791-806. DOI : 10.1080/00263200802285187

Cocugun ne sucu (2012), "Cocugun ne sucu var, anasini kendini oldursun!", *Haberturk Newspaper*. Accessed on 15 September 2012, at http://www.haberturk.com/polemik/haber/747352-cocugun-ne-sucu-var-anasi-kendisini-oldursun-.

Davison, Andrew (2003), "Turkey a 'Secular State'? The Challenge of Description," *South Atlantic Quarterly*, 102(2/3), 333-350. DOI : 10.1215/00382876-102-2-3-333

Dekolte giyene (2011), "Dekolte giyene tecavuz ederler", ntvmsnbc. com. Accessed on 15 September 2012, at http://www.ntvmsnbc. com/id/25182961/.

Delibas, Kayhan (2009), "Conceptualizing Islamic Movements: The Case of Turkey," *International Political Science Review*, 30, 89-103. DOI : 10.1177/0192512108097058

El Guindi, Fadwa (1999), *Veil: Modesty, Privacy and Resistance.* Oxford / New York: Berg.

Entwistle, Joanne (2000), *The Fashioned Body: Fashion, Dress and Modern Social Theory.* Malden, MA: Polity Press.

Fanon, Frantz (1965), *A Dying Colonialism.* New York: Grove Press.

Gokariksel, Banu (2009), "Beyond the Officially Sacred: Religion, Secularism, and the Body in the Production of Subjectivity," *Social and Cultural Geography*, 10(6), 657-674. DOI : 10.1080/14649360903068993

Gokariksel, Banu; Mitchell, Katharyne (2005), "Veiling, Secularism, and the Neoliberal Subject: National Narratives and Supranational Desires in Turkey and France," *Global Networks*, 5(2), 147-165. DOI : 10.1111/j.1471-0374.2005.00112.x

Gokariksel, Banu; Secor, Anna J. (2009), "New Transnational Geographies of Islamism, Capitalism and Subjectivity: The Veiling-Fashion Industry in Turkey," *Area*, 41(1), 6-18. DOI : 10.1111/j.1475-4762.2008.00849.x

Gokariksel, Banu; Secor, Anna (2012), "'Even I Was Tempted': The Moral Ambivalence and Ethical Practice of Veiling-Fashion in Turkey," *Annals of the Association of American Geographers*, 102(4), 1-16. DOI : 10.1080/00045608.2011.601221

Gole, Nilufer (1997), "Secularism and Islamism in Turkey: The Making of Elites and Counter-Elites," *Middle East Journal*, 51(1), 46-58.

Gole, Nilufer (2002), "Islam in Public: New Visibilities and New Imaginaries," *Public Culture*, 14(1), 173-190. DOI : 10.1215/08992363-14-1-173

Gulalp, Haldun (2001), "Globalization and Political Islam: The Social Bases of Turkey's Welfare Party," *International Journal of Middle East Studies*, 33, 433-448. DOI : 10.1017/S0020743801003051

HRW - Human Rights Watch (2011), "'He Loves You, He Beats You.' Family Violence in Turkey and Access to Protection". Accessed on 15 September 2012, at http://www.hrw.org/sites/default/files/ reports/turkey0511webwcover.pdf.

Kandiyoti, Deniz (1997), "Women, Islam and the State," *in* Joel Neinin and Joe Stork (eds.), *Political Islam*. London: I.B. Tauris Publishers.

Keyman, Fuat (2007), "Modernity, Secularism and Islam: The Case of Turkey," *Theory, Culture and Society*, 24(2), 215-234.

Komecoglu, Ugur (2006), "New Sociabilities: Islamic Cafes in Istanbul," *in* Nilüfer Göle and Ludwig Amman (eds.), *Islam in Public: Turkey, Iran and Europe*. Istanbul: Istanbul Bilgi University Press.

Mahmood, Saba (2005), *Politics of Piety: The Islamic Revival and the Feminist Subject*. Princeton, NJ: Princeton University Press.

McKittrick, Kathryn (2006), *Demonic Grounds. Black Women and the Cartographies of Struggle*. Minneapolis: Minnesota University Press.

Mernissi, Fatima (1987), *Beyond the Veil: Male-Female Dynamics in Modern Muslim Society*. Bloomington: Indiana University Press.

Mernissi, Fatima (1991), *The Veil and the Male Elite: A Feminist Interpretation of Women's Rights in Islam*. Cambridge: Perseus Books.

Mernissi, Fatima (2003), "The Meaning of Spatial Boundaries," *in* Reina Lewis and Sara Mills (eds.), *Feminist Postcolonial Theory: A Reader*. New York: Routledge.

Moor, Avigail (2010), "She Dresses to Attract, He Perceives Seduction: A Gender Gap in Attribution of Intent to Women's Revealing Style of Dress and its Relation to Blaming the Victims of Sexual Violence," *Journal of International Women's Studies*, 11(4), 115-127.

Olson, Emelie (1985), "Muslim identity and secularism in contemporary Turkey: 'The Headscarf Dispute,'"*Anthropological Quarterly*, 58(4), 161-171. DOI : 10.2307/3318146

Ozcetin, Hilal (2009), "'Breaking the Silence': The Religious Muslim Women's Movement in Turkey," *Journal of International Women's Studies*, 11(1), 106-119.

Ozdalga, Elizabeth (1998), *The Veiling Issue, Official Secularism and Popular Islam in Modern Turkey*. Richmond, Surrey: Curzon.

Parla, Ayse (2001), "The 'Honor' of the State: Virginity Examinations in Turkey," *Feminist Studies*, 27(1), 65-88. DOI : 10.1525/pol.2000.23.1.185

Polat, Neriman (2012), "Artist Statement" Neriman Polat (personal website). Accessed on 3 October 2012, at http://www.nerimanpolat.com/.

Rhouni, Raja (2009), *Secular and Islamic Feminist Critiques in the Work of Fatima Mernissi*. Leiden, Boston: Brill. DOI : 10.1163/ej.9789004176164.i-296

Sakallioglu, Umit (1996), "Parameters and Strategies of Islam-State Interaction in Republican Turkey," *International Journal of Middle East Studies*, 28(2), 231-251. DOI : 10.1017/S0020743800063157

Saktanber, Ayse (2002), *Living Islam, Women, Religion and Politicization of Culture in Turkey*. London: I.B. Tauris Publishers.

Saktanber, Ayse; Çorbacıoğlu, Gizem (2008), "Veiling and Headscarf – Skepticism in Turkey," *Social Politics*, Winter, 514 538.

Scott, Joan (2007), *Politics of the Veil*. Princeton, NJ: Princeton University Press.

Seckinelgin, Hakan (2006), "Civil Society between the State and Society: Turkish Women with Muslim Headscarves?" *Critical Social Policy*, 26(4), 748-769. DOI : 10.1177/0261018306068472

Secor, Anna (2002), "The Veil and Urban Space in Istanbul: Women's dress, Mobility and Islamic Knowledge," *Gender, Place & Culture*, 9(1), 5-22. DOI : 10.1080/09663690120115010

Sev'er, Aydan; Yurdakul, Gokcecicek (2001), "Culture of Honor, Culture of Change: A Feminist Analysis of Honor Killings in Rural Turkey," *Violence Against Women*, 7, 964-998.

Shirazi, Faegheh. (2001), *The Veil Unveiled: The Hijab in Modern Culture*. Gainesville: University Press of Florida.

Sirman, Nukhet (2004), "Kinship, Politics and Love: Honour in Post-Colonial Contexts – The Case of Turkey," *in* Shahrazad Mojab and Nahla Abdo (eds.), *Violence in the Name of Honour*. Istanbul: Bilgi Üniversitesi Press House, 39-56.

TUIK (2012), Turkish Statistical Institute. Accessed on 15 September 2012, at http://www.tuik.gov.tr/Start.do.

Turbanini cikar (2008), "Turbanini cikar demek donunu cikar demektir" *Hurriyet Newspaper*. Accessed on 15 September 2012, at http://www.hurriyet.com.tr/gundem/8386113.asp.

Universitede artik (2011), "Universitede artik turbana yasak yok" *Radikal Newspaper*. Accessed on 15 September 2012, at http://www.radikal.com.tr/ Radikal.aspx?aType=RadikalDetayV 3&ArticleID=1038728&Date=21.02.2011&CategoryID=86#.

Utku, Hatice Ahsen (2010), "'Collective Privacy' Questioned at C.A.M. Gallery Exhibit," *Today's Zaman*. Accessed on 24 December 2010, at http://www.todayszaman.com/newsDetail_getNewsById.action?newsId=230472.

Uzgel, Ilhan (2003), "Between Praetorianism and Democracy: The Role of the Military in Turkish Foreign Policy," *Turkish Yearbook of International Relations*, 34, 177-212. DOI : 10.1501/Intrel_0000000065

Werbner, Pnina (2007), "Veiled Interventions in Pure Space: Honour, Shame and Embodied Struggles among Muslims in Britain and France," *Theory, Culture and Society*, 24(2), 161-186.

Wolf, Naomi (1997), *The Beauty Myth*. Toronto: Vintage Canada.

Yeğenoğlu, Meyda (1998), *Colonial Fantasies: Towards a Feminist Reading of Orientalism*. New York: Cambridge University Press.

Yeğenoğlu, Meyda (2003), "Veiled fantasies: Cultural and Sexual Difference in the Discourse of Orientalism," in Reina Lewis and Sara Mills (eds.), *Feminist Postcolonial Theory: A Reader*. New York: Routledge, 542-566.

Notes

1. The examples I provide are selections from a wide range of findings based on content research of national news media and social media on the internet for over the period of 2000s. While searching archives of conservative right wing (Zaman, Akit, Yeni Safak) and mainstream (Radikal, Hurriyet, Milliyet) newspapers, as well as social media such as facebook and eksisozluk, I used key words such as "turban", "basortusu" and "turbanli kadin".

16. I am using the term 'veil' here while referring to the works of the authors who have preferred to use it that way. In Turkish context, and throughout the paper, I use the term headscarf (başörtüsü) that is used most generally to refer to the act of covering the head and a form of religious dress.

17. It is noteworthy to emphasize that patriarchal structures constitute the base for not only Islam but all religions, as a main force for shaping social relations and construction of gender identities. However, due to the epistemological standing of Islam as the "other" within the Orientalist Euro-Christian political and social imaginary, gender asymmetries within Islam has always been under the spotlight, as evidenced by the literature I addressed.

18. Religious ruling.

19. A hasema is an Islamic swim suit for women, which covers the whole body and the hair.

Periodical and Internet Sources Bibliography

The following articles have been selected to supplement the diverse views presented in this chapter.

Dan Bilefsky. "How to Avoid Honor Killing in Turkey? Honor Suicide," *The New York Times,* July 16, 2006. http://www.nytimes.com/2006/07/16/world/europe/16turkey.html.

Phylis Collier. "Honor Thy Father," *Off Our Backs,* vol. 37, issue 1, 2007, pp. 12-13.

Adnan R. Khan. "Murdered For Love," *Maclean's,* vol. 118, issue 21, May 23, 2005, pp. 46.

Saira Khan. "The Outrageous "Honor Killing" Of A Pakistani Social-Media Star," *The New Yorker*, July 19, 2016. http://www.newyorker.com/news/news-desk/the-outrageous-honor-killing-of-a-pakistani-social-media-star.

Inna Lazareva. "Unlikely sisters in the Gaza Strip," *New Statesman,* vol. 144, issue 5277, August 28, 2015, pp. 15.

Vanessa Lesnie. "Dying for the Family Honor," *Human Rights,* vol. 27, issue 3, Summer, 2000, pp. 12-14.

Ahmar Mustikhan. "Honour killings," *Canadian Dimension,* vol. 34, issue 1, February 2000, pp. 29.

Rod Nordland. "In Spite of the Law, Afghan 'Honor Killings' Of Women Continue," *New York Times,* vol. 163, issue 56491, pp. 10. https://www.nytimes.com/2014/05/04/world/asia/in-spite-of-the-law-afghan-honor-killings-of-women-continue.html.

GLOBALVIEWPOINTS

CHAPTER 2

The Cultural Origins
of Honor Killing

Violence Against Women Is Rooted in Patriarchy

Charles Recknagel

In the following viewpoint, Radio Free Europe/Radio Liberty writer Charles Recknagel argues that honor crimes are not religiously based. Recknagel notes that in addition to inflexible attitudes about women's roles, and enforced patriarchal roles, economic factors also contribute to the occurrence of honor crimes. Besides being hidden from police, honor crimes are viewed by the communities in which they occur as upholding traditional values.

As you read, consider the following questions:

1. According to Recknagel, what are two reasons why the statistical number of reported honor killings probably is much higher?
2. From where do experts believe the notion of familial honor arises?
3. How do economic factors feed into the practice of honor killing?

I n some societies, it is common for men to think of wives and daughters as both assets and liabilities. So long as they are obedient to their fathers and husbands, they are a source of pride.

But if they disobey and show independence, they become a source of shame and may even be murdered to protect the family's "honor."

Here are five things to know about "honor killings" and why they are so hard to stop.

How Frequent Are Honor Crimes?

According to UN statistics available, some 5,000 honor killings a year are reported worldwide. But many experts believe the real number is much higher because many honor crimes are often hidden from the police.

The hiding of honor crimes is possible because they often take place within a family. Leading members, including females, decide that the woman or girl who has compromised the family's honor must be put to death. The crime is kept secret through a code of silence.

Jacqueline Thibault, whose Swiss-based association Surgir protects potential victims of honor killings in the Middle East, says murders are often reported as suicides. In some cases, there is no "need" for a murder because the family pressure is so great that the victim commits suicide herself.

Are Honor Crimes Unique to the Muslim World?

No, honor crimes are found in many parts of the globe and are not tied to any single religion. Countries where they take place are as diverse as Brazil and India, Pakistan and Albania. However, they occur with the greatest frequency in the Middle East and South Asia and only sparingly in South America and Central Asia, as well as among some immigrant populations in Europe.

"Honor crimes tend to happen in places where there are inflexible and discriminatory attitudes about women's roles, especially around their sexuality, and these are often applicable to women but not exclusively so, because sometimes men are targeted for honor crimes as well," says Rothna Begum, Middle East and North Africa researcher for Human Rights Watch (HRW).

"Women or couples seen as having brought dishonor on the community or family face violence, which is then held out as a chilling example for others."

Experts say that honor killings are linked to patriarchal societies and the earliest historical evidence of them dates back to Babylon. They arise from the notion that women are the vessels of a family's honor and are closely tied to values placed on marriage with virgin brides. Under this concept of honor, a family's inability to guarantee a daughter's virginity prior to marriage is a cause for shame and for ostracism by neighbors.

But there are also economic factors at work.

Thibault says that in societies that practice arranged marriages, unions are as much about ensuring the common interests of the two families as those of the betrothed.

"These are marriages between families much more than between a man and a woman and marriages between families are to obtain a better economic situation, to get more farmland, to have a better social standing," says Thibault. "If the marriage is threatened or broken off, the family no longer attains what it hoped for in terms of better social or economic status."

Why Are Laws Alone Insufficient to Protect Victims?

Honor killings are illegal around the world, but many legal systems are lenient with those who commit them because the perpetrators are seen by the society as defending traditional values.

The leniency shows up in legal loopholes that allow killers to go free. One common loophole is a provision that allows the victim's closet kin to forgive the killer.

"Because the victim is killed by the family themselves, the family is able to forgive the family member who killed the wife, or daughter, or sister," says Begum. "So you are in a situation where the murderer gets away with it."

Some murders occur even after the girl has left her family, but the loopholes still apply. The killer can ask forgiveness from the husband's family and hope social pressure will ensure he gets it. He can also hope the other family will accept monetary compensation, or "blood money," for the crime so that he is spared punishment.

How Do Potential Victims of Honor Killings Protect Themselves?

Because victims are targeted by their own families, protection is very difficult. Just how difficult can be measured by the fact that in some countries, including Jordan and Afghanistan, potential victims sometimes seek refuge in prisons where, despite being incarcerated, they are at least beyond their families' reach.

However, Thibault notes that women cannot simply ask to be put in jail. The legal system requires they be guilty of a crime, so the girls first confess to a misdemeanor they have not committed.

Once in prison, the girls may hope that over time their families may agree to take them back or not to track them down after they are released. But Thibault, whose organization tries to mediate family reunions in Jordan, says there is never any certainty of forgiveness.

"Our social workers mediate with the families to see if the families will accept them back despite everything," she says. "In some cases, very few, the families accept, but one can never be sure that it will last and that the family won't kill her two months later. Each case has to be followed very closely."

Are Honor Crimes on Their Way Out?

Honor crimes have existed in societies where they no longer exist today, including in remote rural areas of Greece and southern Italy as recently as the early decades of the last century. But experts say they are hard to eradicate unless laws against them are strictly enforced.

"It really comes down to how the laws are being implemented and changed," says Begum. "In countries where they continue to have mitigating circumstances or offenses that allow for the

Honor Killing Is Prevalent in Islamic Cultures

AP recently lied: "The killers routinely invoke Islam, but rarely can they cite anything other than their belief that Islam doesn't allow the mixing of sexes. Even Pakistan's hard-line Islamic Ideology Council, which is hardly known for speaking out to protect women, says the practice defies Islamic tenets."

Here is the reality: Muslims commit 91 percent of honor killings worldwide. The Palestinian Authority gives pardons or suspended sentences for honor murders. Iraqi women have asked for tougher sentences for Islamic honor murderers, who get off lightly now. Syria in 2009 scrapped a law limiting the length of sentences for honor killings, but "the new law says a man can still benefit from extenuating circumstances in crimes of passion or honour 'provided he serves a prison term of no less than two years in the case of killing.'" And in 2003 the Jordanian Parliament voted down on Islamic grounds a provision designed to stiffen penalties for honor killings. Al-Jazeera reported that "Islamists and conservatives said the laws violated religious traditions and would destroy families and values."

Until the encouragement Islamic law gives to honor killing is acknowledged and confronted, more women will be victimized.

"Honour Killing Bill against Islam," The News International, October 8, 2016:

> Jamaat-e-Islami ameer Senator Siraj-ul-Haq on Friday said Imam Hussain (RA)'s mission was the establishment of the rule of law with equal rights for all citizens, a system based on Shoora (consultation).
>
> In a country established for Islam, the rulers had thrust a system based on tyranny and exploitation, exactly opposite to the message of Karbala which was to fight against oppression and tyranny, he said while delivering Friday sermon at Mansoora Masjid. Siraj-ul-Haq said the passage of a so-called Honour Killing Bill by the joint session of the parliament in conflict with Quran and Sunnah proved that the ruling party was out to demolish the ideological boundaries of the country.
>
> He said denying the right of compromise to the parties in the cases of honour killings was repugnant to divine injunctions, and added that any law in conflict with the Shariah would not be tolerated. Siraj-ul-Haq pointed out that PPP's founder ZA Bhutto had never imposed his socialist ideology on the country.

- *"Pakistan: Muslim leader says bill against honor killing is un-Islamic," by Robert Spencer, Jihad Watch, 10/9/16.*

offenders to be pardoned, there is no deterrent and it sends a message to society that it is OK to kill the women of their families if they breach their honor."

In the most recent case in Pakistan, where Farzana Parveen was bludgeoned to death on May 26 by members of her family for marrying a man of her own choice, her husband, Muhammad Iqbal, has himself told reporters that he strangled his first wife so he could marry Farzana. The fact that he escaped punishment for that crime only to lose his next wife to an honor killing underlines the revolving-door nature of laws that are not enforced.

Khawar Mumtaz, chairwoman of Pakistan's National Commission on the Status of Women, says her commission is aware that the loopholes in the law are abused and wants them closed.

"There is a loophole in our law under which the affected families forgive the killers [through a mutual compromise]," Mumtaz says. "But there is also another section 311 in the Penal Code under which such people could be punished [but which] is usually not applied in the first investigation report. We are trying to apply this so that the family's pardon does not help [the accused]."

Islam Forbids Honor Killing

Jonathan Brown

In the following viewpoint, Georgetown University chair of Islamic civilization Jonathan Brown asserts that honor killings are neither caused nor encouraged by Islam. Though detractors of the religion contend that Islam and the laws of Muslim countries are lax on offenders, Brown identifies French and British criminal law codes as the basis of those nations' modern legal systems.

As you read, consider the following questions:

1. According to Brown, what serious consequences arise from attributing honor killing solely to Islam?
2. What type of violence against women far outnumbers honor killing?
3. What clear position does Brown contend that Shariah law has on honor killing?

T his is part of the history of honor killings you're unlikely to read or hear about. In 1947 in the British colony of Nigeria, English judges had to overturn what they viewed as the backwards ruling of a local Shariah court. A man had been sentenced to death for murder, but the British superior court pointed out that it had been a crime of passion. The man had killed his wife's lover. The Shariah court had been unimpressed by this excuse, but the British court decided that the murderer did not deserve to die.[1]. Yes, you read that

"Islam is not the cause of Honor Killings. It's part of the solution," by Jonathan Brown, Yaqeen Institute for Islamic Research, October 25, 2016. Reprinted by permission.

correctly. A Shariah court, applying Shariah law, did not buy the "crime of passion" argument that has long served as a justification for honor killings. The British court did.

Honor killings are never far from the headlines. The Islamophobic Clarion Fund even released a documentary called *Honor Diaries*, which repeats the accusation that Islam supports honor killings and that these acts of violence are endemic to Muslim societies.

But the truth of the matter is that honor killings are not caused or encouraged by Islam. Honor killing, despite the popular rhetoric around it, is not even a problem specific to Muslims[2]. Its most concentrated and serious occurrences don't involve Muslims at all. This ignorance about Islam's teachings and the realities of violence against women has serious costs. First, blaming honor crimes on Islam antagonizes Muslims unnecessarily. It feeds the narrative, prevalent in many Muslim countries, that dismisses human rights as a proxy for Westernization and cultural imperialism. Second, sensationalism over Islam deflects from a reality that many men are loath to admit: that violence against women is a global problem with roots much deeper than the doctrines of one religion or the features of one culture. It needs to be addressed as such. Finally, obsessing over Islam's alleged acceptance of honor crimes blinds Muslims and non-Muslims to the condemnation of these crimes in Muhammad's teachings and the Shariah.

The tragedy of violence directed at women because they are women is far too widespread and long-lived to be the product of any one religion or even one culture. Though it takes different shapes and appears with varied frequency from region to region, it afflicts all societies. Patriarchal societies (i.e., all societies to one degree or another) sometimes "justify" some of this violence as the consequence of rage triggered in "crimes of passion." Other forms of violence against women, such as honor killings, can involve premeditation and even the coordination of several people, including women related to the victim. In those parts of the world plagued worst by violence against women, legal systems tend to offer official or unofficial leniency for the men who commit it.

Honor crimes are only part of the larger phenomenon of *femicide,* or the murder of a woman for some reason associated with her gender. The women and girls who are the victims of such violence are attacked because they are perceived to have violated some profound expectation of how women are supposed to act in their society. In the Mediterranean region, especially the Middle East and North Africa, as well as South Asia, affronts are to the "honor" of the woman or her family. The United Nations Population Fund (UNFPA) has conservatively estimated that at least 5,000 women a year globally are victims of honor killings. In India and Pakistan, this often entails a daughter or sister being killed for falling in love with a man without parental approval and occurs amongst Hindu and Muslim populations alike. Femicide takes other forms elsewhere. A 2012 UN report details how in parts of southern Africa, South and Southeast Asia hundreds of women are killed each year after being accused of witchcraft. Their killers receive lighter sentences with alarming regularity.

Despite the media attention they receive, honor killings are not the most prevalent type of femicide. The number of honor killings, whether in Muslim countries or elsewhere, pales in comparison with the most serious form of violence against women, namely dowry killings among India's Hindu population. Dowry killings, the murder of a wife by her husband or his family, often by burning, for her failure to provide a large enough dowry payment to her husband's family, ceasing dowry gifts or merely for falling short of expectations in her wifely duties, have occurred in shocking numbers. A 2012 UN report observed that 8,383 known dowry murders occurred in India in 2009, up from 4,836 in 1990. Though the Indian government outlawed dowry giving decades ago and identified dowry murders as a criminal problem, dowry giving remains an important custom and the suspicious death of wives is rarely investigated. The police often dismiss these deaths as kitchen accidents.

Islamophobic organizations point out that Islam and the laws of Muslim countries excuse honor killings or treat them lightly. On the second point they are correct. Such laws are a problem, and one that seems to have proliferated in the Middle East. In Egyptian law, a man who kills his wife and/or her lover after catching them "in the act" (in flagrante delicto) is only punished with prison as opposed to the death penalty. Morocco, Kuwait, Lebanon, Syria, Yemen, Oman, the UAE, and Jordan's laws extend drastically reduced penalties for the murder of any female relative (and their lover) that a man finds in such a situation (though the UAE and a 2001 update to Jordan's laws allows the same excuse for a woman who finds her husband in bed with another woman).

But none of these laws has any basis in the Shariah or Islamic teachings. In fact, they were originally imported from the West. Criminal law in the Middle East today was shaped by the Ottoman Criminal Code of 1858, which was issued as part of the failing Ottoman Empire's efforts to imitate its European rivals. The Code was little more than a translation of the French Criminal Code of 1832, copying word for word its lax punishment for honor crimes. This is still evident today in the laws of Lebanon, Syria, Jordan and to a lesser extent Morocco (never part of the Ottoman Empire), which read like literal translations from the French. The French and Ottoman law codes also served as the major inspiration for Egypt's law as well.

In Pakistan, another country regularly in the news over honor crimes, we find a similar case with British law. Despite having a legal system influenced by the Shariah, Pakistan's criminal law remains based in the 1860 code that the British imported to rule colonial India. This law granted leniency to a husband who killed his wife due to "grave and sudden provocation." Pakistan reformed this law in 1990, ironically, in an attempt to bring the country's laws closer in accord with the Shariah. In particular, Pakistan's Federal Shariat Court declared that, "according to the teachings of Islam, provocation, no matter how grave and sudden it is, does not lessen the intensity of crime of murder" (sic). Sadly, Pakistani courts sometimes still hand down reduced punishments for the men who commit honor killings. But the judges who do so have justified this by once again citing the "grave and sudden provocation" suffered by the murderer—the exact wording of the British law[3].

Shariah law has a clear position on honor killing, drawing directly on rulings made by the Prophet Muhammad: a husband who kills his wife and/or her lover has committed homicide like any other case, even if the husband caught the two in the act. The basis of this comes from Hadiths, or sayings of the Prophet Muhammad. When he was asked what would happen if a husband found his wife with another man, the Prophet responded that the husband could not kill him and that no one could be punished unless the husband brought four witnesses who had seen the act[4]. The Quran set down the practical procedure for husbands or wives who suspected infidelity as well as those who caught their spouse cheating but had no witnesses: the couple would appear before a judge, and the accusing spouse would swear to God five times that their accusation was true. If the accused spouse then swore five times to God that they were innocent, neither party was punished but the couple was divorced (Quran 24:6-7).

Muslim scholars have been well aware of the dangers of violence against women. The famous nineteenth-century Yemeni scholar al-Shawkānī (d. 1834 CE) wrote that one of the reasons that men who murder women are liable to be executed is the phenomenon of male violence against women for supposed slights of honor. He concluded that, "There is no doubt that laxity on this matter is one of the greatest means leading to women's lives being destroyed, especially in the Bedouin regions, which are characterized by harsh-heartedness and a strong sense of honor and shame stemming from Pre-Islamic times."[5]

The foreignness of honor killing to the Shariah is so clear that, for centuries, Muslim legal scholars have been in substantial agreement on the issue*. In fact, when confronted with a report that the early caliph Umar had ruled that men who killed wives they found engaged in adultery would not be punished, Muslim scholars could only conclude that he must have meant that they would not be punished by God in the Afterlife. In this life, the Shariah was clear that they were murderers[6]. In the modern period, many of the most prominent muslim scholars from all sects and backgrounds, such as the Sunnis Yūsuf al-Qaraḍāwī and ʿAbdallāh al-Ghumārī (d. 1993) and the late Shiite scholar Muḥammad Ḥusayn Faḍlāllāh (d. 2010), have declared honor killing totally impermissible in Islam, as have a group of Canadian imams, the Muslim Council of Britain and the prominent American imam Zaid Shakir.

We can continue to rehash the tired line of Islam allowing honor killing. Or we can point out that the Prophet's teachings and the Shariah condemn the act in no uncertain terms. Violence against women and the failure of legal systems to punish it is a serious problem in Muslim countries like Afghanistan and Pakistan. Islam and the Shariah should be mobilized as arguments against this rather than as its supposed causes. The number of dowry killing amongst Hindus in India alone dwarfs honor killings globally, and the country that ranks worst in the UN's rankings of femicide is the decidedly non-Shariah applying, majority Catholic El Salvador. These realities, along with the fact that the laws in Muslim countries that indulge honor killings are actually imported from Europe, should remind us of something our society conveniently overlooks: violence against women is mankind's problem, and it's as much a part of the past and present of the West as anywhere else.

*   * There is one glaring exception to the overall rejection of honor killing in the Shariah tradition. Law in the Ottoman Empire created a space for the practice on the basis of a bizarre inversion of the Prophet's ruling on the question. In one of the Hadiths, the Prophet explains that killing an adulterous spouse could only be legitimate if there were four witnesses to her adultery, since this was the evidence required for normally convicting someone of adultery. Instead of understanding this as a far-fetched and nigh impossible condition (since there would have to be four, upstanding male witnesses who had all seen actual penetration occur), some Ottoman jurists used*

it to wedge in laxity over honor killings. Even then, however, there were limits. Ottoman law only exonerated men who had killed their wives or daughters, and it only applied in situations in which the man killed the male lover to prevent him from completing an act in progress. This would actually violate the understanding of the Prophet's command as explained by Saʿd b. ʿUbāda, who, although he was initially against the Prophet's ruling because of his pride and honor, then said that, if he found a man with his wife, he would "not even move him until I had brought four witnesses. And, by God, I would not bring them until that man had finished."[7] The unusual Ottoman permissiveness regarding honor killings would explain why the Empire adopted the French law permitting it in 1858.

Footnotes

1. Rudolph Peters, Crime and Punishment in Classical Islamic Law (Cambridge: Cambridge University Press, 2005), 124..

2. It has been found that, in upper Egypt, Coptic families are as likely as Muslims to commit honor killing; Recep Dogan, "Is Honour Killing a 'Muslim Phenomenon'? Textual Interpretation and Cultural Representations," Journal of Muslim Minority Affairs 31, no. 3 (2011): 423-440.

3. Sohail Akbar Warraich, "'Honor Killings' and the law in Pakistan," in 'Honour': Crimes, Paradigms, and Violence against Women, ed. Lynn Welchmann and Sara Hossain (London: Zed Books, 2005), 84-97.

4. The main Hadiths are those of Abū Hurayra in which Saʿd b. ʿUbāda asks the Prophet, "What do you think if I found a man with my wife? Should I wait until I bring four witnesses? (a-raʾayta in wajadtu maʿa imraʾatī rajulan a-umhiluhu ḥattā ātiya bi-arbaʿat shuhadāʾ)." The Prophet replies, "Yes." See Ṣaḥīḥ Muslim: kitāb al-liʿān; Sunan Abī Dāwūd: kitāb al-diyāt, bāb man wajada maʿa ahlihi rajulan a-yaqtuluhu. See also Mālik's Muwaṭṭaʾ: kitāb al-aqḍiya, bāb man wajada maʿa imraʾatihi rajulan; Musnad Aḥmad Ibn Ḥanbal (Maymaniyya print), 1:238-39.

5. Muḥammad b. ʿAlī al-Shawkānī, Nayl al-Awṭār, ed. ʿIzz al-Dīn Khaṭṭāb, 8 vols. (Beirut: Dār Iḥyāʾ al-Turāth al-ʿArabī, 2001), 7:24.

6. Abū Sulaymā Ḥamd al-Khaṭṭābī, Maʿālim al-sunan, 3rd ed., 4 vols. (Beirut: al-Maktaba al-ʿIlmiyya, 1981), 4:19; al-Suyūṭī, al-Ashbāh waʾl- naẓāʾir, ed. Muḥammad al-Muʿtaṣim al-Baghdādī (Beirut: Dār al-Kitāb al-ʿArabī, 1414/1993), 746.

7. Musnad Ibn Ḥanbal, 1:238

Honor Killing Runs Rampant in Islamic Cultures

Peter Pilt

In the following viewpoint, Peter Pilt argues that Westerners cannot appreciate the true meaning of living as part of a community as do those raised under traditional Islamic culture. He claims that Westerners are individualistic whereas individuals in Islamic culture gain identity through social groups based on an honor-shame culture. Pilt, an international director of Global Care in Gold Coast, Australia, cites that these individuals gain success by fulfilling social group expectations grounded in the Quran.

As you read, consider the following questions:

1. What is the difference between honor killing and honor crimes as reported by the author?
2. How is an individual ostracized, according to Pilt, when they do not conform to the norms of Muslim society?
3. As stated by the author, how does the Quran view women?

Introduction

The thesis of this paper is to examine the claim that the gender issue of Honour Killings is rooted in Islam. It will propose a definition and look at the extent of honour killings, with specific stories from various countries. This paper will specifically hone in on

"Honour Killings—Are they rooted in Islam?" by Peter Pilt, November 28, 2013. Reprinted by permission.

the question, is there a basis for honour killings in the writings of the Qu'ran, Hadith or other Islamic writings? Additionally the general treatment of women by Islam will be discussed, looking to see if the teachings of Islam toward women set an atmosphere that is conducive to the flourishing of the killing of female family members. Prior to drawing the paper together in an action orientated conclusion, the paper will look at the missiological response of Christians to Honour Killings.

What Is Honour Killing?

Honour killings are murders that take place generally by family members and perpetrated on, in the main, females. Fadia Faqir in his article Intrafamily Femicide:in Defence of Honour, defines them as "the killing of women for suspected deviation from sexual norms imposed by society" (Faqir 2001:66). But it is more than the deviation from sexual norms—honour killings happen when these deviations are thought to bring shame upon a family. But it doesn't even have to have occurred. Veena Meetoo and Heidi Mirza writing for the Social Policy Research centre at Middlesex University, says "Being suspected of sexual deviancy such as pregnancy outside of marriage or adulterous behaviour is also seen as enough to justify punishing a women" (Meeton V. Mirza H. 2007:187). Honour killings are specific to honour/shame based cultures or religions: Manar Hason writing in the *Journal of Israeli History: Politics, Society, Culture* in an article titled The Politics of Honour, identifies the fact that when we speak of honour in an honour killing context it is referring to the honour of the family as a patriarchal unit. Honour he says "refers chiefly to the honour of males in the family: The maintenance of honour is the perpetuation of male control: an assault on honour undermines that system of domination" (Manar Hasan 2002:3). Although the focus of this paper is honour killings, there is a term Honour Crimes, that is closely related but broader than just killings. Ferri K Nesheiwat writing in the Penn State International Law Review says that the "condoned violence that exists under the Honour Crime umbrella includes murder, attempted murder, acid attacks and female infanticides" (Nesheiwat F. 2004:54). In 2000, the United Nations estimated that there were 5000 honour killings a year (United Nations Population Fund, 2000: 56), but Phyllis Chesler writing in the *Middle East Quarterly*, estimates that there would be that many women killed in Pakistan each year alone (Chesler 2010:3). The number is hard to ascertain as one of the characteristics of Honour Killings, is that they often go unreported.

Honour Killings are on the increase and "have accelerated significantly in a 20 year period between 1989 and 2009" (Chesler 2010:4). The world wide average age of victims of Honour Killings is 23 leading to the conclusion that this is a crime against young women. "Just over half of these victims were daughters or sisters and a about a quarter were wives or girlfriends, of the perpetrators" (Chesler 2010:4). Here are some very sad statistics:—

- 72% of victims were killed by members of their family of origin.

- 42% of victims were killed by multiple perpetrators.

- Worldwide, more than 50% were tortured, which includes being raped or gang-raped before being killed, being strangled or bludgeoned to death, being stabbed multiple times, being burned, stoned to death or beheaded (Chesler 2010:5).

Whilst Honour Killings are generally around immorality, adultery or rumoured immorality, there are stories of girls being killed for simply walking towards a house where single men lived, going for a walk without a father's permission or dressing in jeans.

Honour Killing Stories

Pakistan: Two teenage girls aged 15 and 16 were shot dead by their step brother after a video of them dancing in the rain was circulated. The step brother, Khutore, during the investigation said he "considered the video an assault on the honour of his family" (Ron Crilly, *The Telegraph* 1st July 2013).

Yemen: According to the Examiner.com website—A father has just been arrested for burning his 15 year old daughter to death for speaking to her fiancé before their wedding day. He was quoted as saying that his daughter "had shamed the family with un-islamic behaviour."

Iraq: Shyamalie Satkunanandan writing about honour killings in Iraq reports on the Wadi Online website: In February of this year, Sakas Hamadamin, a 28 year old school teacher, was shot and killed by her father for wanting to marry a man deemed unsuitable.

America. Reporting on CBSnews.com, Lisa Freed and Jonathan Leach report: 20 year old college student Noor Almaleki was run over and killed by her father because he disapproved of her lifestyle.

Is There a Basis for Honour Killings in the Writings of the Qu'ran, Hadith?

First as a Westerner, we must understand that we see the world very differently to people who have been raised in a traditional Islamic culture. Our framework is very individualistic, where we see ourselves as being the complete controllers of our lives. We don't grasp the reality of what it means to live in community and the breakdown of the family means that we no longer even really grasp what it means to be part of a functioning, healthy family. We like the idea that we are accountable to no one and the increasingly secularisation of western neo liberal democracies means that we have tricked ourselves into believing we are not even accountable to a higher authority such as God. Christine Mallouhi in her book Miniskirts, Mothers and Muslims says "Much of the failure of Westerners to grasp the underlying premises of Muslim culture results from our failure to understand and appreciate Muslim self perception" (Mallouhi 2004:21). Mallouhi identifies in her exposition of Islamic culture that unlike the West, "Islamic culture is deeply based on honour and shame" (Mallouhi 2004:23). Nesheiwat in the Penn State International Law Review says "In Islamic and Middle Eastern societies a distinct honor-shame culture exists wherein individuals derive their identity from their social group, especially their family and kinship network. The individual's success is gauged by fulfillment of that social group's expectations" (Nesheiwat F. 2004:55). Mallouhi makes the observation that "the central premises of the Muslim world is one of right conduct quoting from the Qu'ran '*You are the best community that hath been raised up for mankind. Ye enjoin right conduct and forbid indecency, and ye believe in Allah 3:110*'" (Mallouhi 2004: 22). She concludes by saying that "a good image is very important in Muslim culture" (Mallouhi 2004:35).

To not conform to the norms of Muslim society is to be ostracized: which has tremendous economic and social implications. These economic and social implications add to the religious and cultural pressures already in the honour/shame mix, leading to honour killings not just being made in the name of Allah, but also in the name of Mammon. "Dishonour can so totally undermine a family's economic status by ruining a husband's reputation or the marital prospects of sons, that mothers sometimes do not interfere with the abuse or murder of their daughters" (Meeton V. Mirza H. 2007:191). Redjeb Tutku in a Dissertation, Violence Against Women: Turkey and the Economics of Honour Killings says that "virginity has become a valuable commodity that can be transferred from father to husband for a price" (Tutku 2013:47). Obviously then the pressure to guard this economic asset is significant and so fathers guard and brood over their daughters to ensure no flirting, no dressing inappropriately, no being soiled by westernisation and absolutely no falling in love and marrying the "wrong man"

One only has to take a casual look at the locations of Honour Killings to quickly jump to the conclusion that they are obviously deeply rooted in the Islamic world. In fact WikiIslam, The Online Resource for Muslims says that 91% of honour killings around the entire world are carried out by Muslims. Why are honour killings so prevalent in the Islamic world when the Qu'ran doesn't specifically condone them? I will point out here that stoning of adulterers has been part of Sharia law every since the wife of the

Prophet Muhammad, Aisha, claimed that a goat inadvertently ate up the Qur'anic verse sanctioning the stoning to death of a woman. It is worth noting here however, that there were no cases or honour killings in the early period of Islam according to the website Questions about Islam. There are however a number of verses that are used to provide Qu'ranic or Hadithic license for honour killings. These were all taken off the Answering Islam Website.

Surah 18, Al-Kahf (The Cave), verses 66 —84, mentions that a boy was killed because he was about to bring his parents grief and dishonour through his unbelief. Muslim commentators are not in agreement whether the servant of Allah who murdered the boy was an angel or a prophet. The important fact is that Allah wanted him to be dead because the boy would bring future dishonour to them.

Surah 24, An-Nur, verse 2, the punishment for adultery is 100 stripes, but this is actually contrary to hadiths found in Sahih Bukhari, 2.413, 8.805, 814, and 819, where it is stoning to death.

Surah 4, An-Nisā' (The Women), verses 34-35 state that men are in charge of women, being their protectors and maintainers. This sense of ownership and the pressure from Islamic culture to conform to social norms means that when a women steps out of line, there must be the resulting punishment.

Surah 4, An Nisa Verse 15 *"If any of your women are guilty of lewdness, take the evidence of four (reliable) witnesses from amongst you against them; if they testify, confine them to houses until death do claim them. Or God ordain for them some (other) way."*

Surah 17, Al-Isra (The Night Journey) Verse 32 *" Nor come nigh to adultery: for it is a shameful (deed) and an evil, opening the road (to other evils).*

Surah AL –Ahzab (The Combined Forces) Verse 33 *"stay quietly in your houses, and make not a dazzling display."*

Hadith—Sahi Bukhari: 8:6814:

Narrated Jabir bin Abdullah al-Ansari: "A man from the tribe of Bani Aslam came to Allah's Messenger [Muhammad] and informed him that he had committed illegal sexual intercourse;

and he bore witness four times against himself. Allah's Messenger ordered him to be stoned to death as he was a married person."

Sahi Muslim No. 4206:

A woman came to the prophet and asked for purification by seeking punishment. He told her to go away and seek God's forgiveness. She persisted four times and admitted she was pregnant. He told her to wait until she had given birth. Then he said that the Muslim community should wait until she had weaned her child. When the day arrived for the child to take solid food, Muhammad handed the child over to the community. And when he had given command over her and she was put in a hole up to her breast, he ordered the people to stone her. Khalid b. al-Walid came forward with a stone which he threw at her head, and when the blood spurted on her face he cursed her.

Al-Bayhaqi:

The Prophet (peace and blessings be upon him) said, "O mankind! Beware of fornication/adultery for it entails six dire consequences: three of them relating to this world and three to the next world. As for the three that are related to this world, they are the following: it removes the glow of one's face, brings poverty, and reduces the life-span. As for its dire consequences in the next world they are: it brings down the wrath of Allah upon the person, subjects him to terrible reckoning, and finally casts him in hell-fire.

Women and Islam—Negative

There are additional factors that have led to honour killings being an increasing part of Islam. Phyllis Chesler writing in the *Middle East Quarterly* in an article titled World Wide Trends in Honour Killings, identifies a number of these factors: "normalised child abuse including arranged marriages, sexual repression, gender separatism and the demands made by an increase in the violent theology of jihad" (Chesler 2010:7). The general way women are seen by Islam, I believe also contributes to the ease in which they are disposed of when they wander outside of the very strict sexual norms of Islamic society. Chesler called this "the devaluation of women and girls" (Chesler 2010:7). In Khaled Hosseini's soul-piercing novel about life in Islamic Afghanistan, *A Thousand Splendid Suns*, the character Nana, a poor unwed mother, tells her five-year-old daughter, Mariam: "Learn this now and learn it well, my daughter: Like a compass needle that points north, a man's accusing finger always finds a woman. Always. You remember that, Mariam" (Hosseini 2007:7). Whether this negative view of women was the intention or not of the Prophet Mohammed the Hadiths that have arisen around Islam certainly interpret his writing that way. Before that issue is dealt with, I will suggest some Qu'ranic verses that do lean toward the conclusion that women are inferior, owned by men or need to be controlled. I will provide counter arguments though to bring a balanced analysis to this.

The Qur'an's account of creation indicate that women are inferior to men as they were taken out of men—so males are the fullness of the creation and women are like a second generation photocopy of the original: Not quite the same quality. (Surah 7:189, 39:6). Melanie Adrian writing in the *Journal of Muslim Minority Affairs* has a counter opinion "Though Qur'anic verse 4:1 (Surah An-Nisa-Women) and Qur'anic verse 7:20–22 (Surah Al-A'raf—The Heights) are explicit about how human beings were created and how the first sin was committed, the story has often been used wrongly to portray women as inferior to men, a second sex and also sinners from birth" (*Adrian* Vol. 31, No. 3, September 2011:16).

Professor Evelyne Reisacher, the Associate Professor of Islamic Studies at Fuller Theological Seminary, in discussing Amina Wadud's position on this issue in her book *Qur'an and Women*, says "Wadud contends that Sura 4:1 and other similar verses (Sura 7:189) show that men and women were created from the same soul (*nafs wahidan*), same essence and therefore they are equal in the eyes of God. Other scholars like Rifat Hassan, Namet Hafez Barazangi or Nurjannah Ismail make the same claim. They believe that male and female were created from the same soul in pairs. This interpretation opposes female subordination." (Week 2 Posting for MR557).

The Qur'an uses a possessive construct when talking about women, meaning they are possessions of men (Wadud 1999:32), and always when speaking of a woman links her to a man (Wadud 1999:33). In Qur'anic verse 4:5 (Surah An-Nisa-Women), it says *"Do not give the feeble-minded the property with which God has entrusted you for their support; but maintain and clothe them with its proceeds, and speak kind words to them."*

Voula Papas writing an article titled Islam and Women's Rights for the Atheist Foundation of Australia's website, sums up her assessment of how women are treated by Islam by saying:-

> *Under the Shari'a, compensation for the murder of a woman is half the amount of that of a man. A woman's testimony in court is worth only half of a man's. Women are entitled to only half the inheritance of males; the reason given for these is that males have families to provide for. In sura 4:34 men are granted superiority and authority over women because they spend their wealth to maintain them, this implies that women are a burden on society and that their work in caring for children, household and livestock is insignificant and trivial.*

In the Islamic world, scholars come out very strong in support of honour killings. *Syed* Kamran Mirza writing in a blog article titled Honor Killing is Absolutely Islamic, quotes the following Scholars:-

> *Sheikh Ahmad Kutty, a senior lecturer and Islamic scholar at the Islamic Institute of Toronto, Ontario, Canada, states: "Adultery in Islam is one of the most heinous and deadliest of sins. Its enormity can be gauged from the fact that it has often been conjoined in the Qur'an with the gravest of all sins: shirk or associating partners with Allah."*
>
> *The Saudi Ambassador to London, Ghazi al-Qusaibi, says that stoning may seem irrational to the western mind, but it is "at the core of the Islamic faith." An intellectual, the Saudi ambassador to London asserted that stoning adulterers to death is a legitimate punishment for society. He also says that Westerners should respect Muslim culture on this matter.*

Women and Islam—Positive

Further to Islam's treatment of women, Muhammad is reputed to have said that he had had a glimpse of Hell and that most of its occupants were women. Tradition in Islam also holds that women have 9 times the sex drive of men, which means they need to be controlled. This is one of mentalities that have seen Female Genital Mutilation (FGM), which is basically the removal of the clitoris as it is seen as the centre of a women's sex drive, having such a strong hold in Islamic countries. FGM pre dates Islam but Islam now has adopted it as "the right Islamic thing to do." I would transition this paper at this juncture by saying what Islam has done to FGM, it has also done to Honour Killings. The website All About Muhammad: Women Under Islam makes the following observation about Muhammad,

> *"In his day, Muhammad would have been considered as one of the foremost advocates of women's rights. In the 7th Century, before he gained control of the Arabian Peninsula, women of the region had even fewer rights than Muslim women today. Female babies were often buried alive, spousal abuse was the norm and women had no rights of inheritance. After revelations from Allah (Muhammad), infanticide was prohibited, spousal abuse was codified, and a female inheritor could obtain half that of a male beneficiary."*

Christianity and Honour Killings

To assist in the journey of discovery as to whether Honour Killings were rooted in Islam or more in Arabic Culture, I remembered some uncomfortable biblical scriptures that seemingly encourage honour killings.

Death for Adultery: *If a man commits adultery with another man's wife, both the man and the woman must be put to death. (Leviticus 20:10 NLT)*

Death for Fornication *A priest's daughter who loses her honour by committing fornication and thereby dishonours her father also, shall be burned to death.(Leviticus 21:9 NAB)..*

We could also conclude that the very first example of an honour killing, although not involving the death of a human, was when Adam and Eve found themselves shamed and naked because of their sin and God killed an animal in order to restore their honour by taking away their shame. Genesis 3:21 *Also for Adam and his wife the Lord God made tunics of skin, and clothed them.* Was there a precedent set right there in the Garden, that the shedding of blood restores honour? Was this precedent followed when Jesus died on the cross? In other words, is Jesus' death an honour killing.

Reality is, Christian's aren't killing their wives when they commit adultery!

Honour Killings Rooted in Culture

A.J. Almaney writing in the *Management International Review* in an article tilted Cultural Traits of the Arabs, cites a myth about Arab culture that "there are no common cultural traits among the Arabs and that there is no such thing as an "Arab Personality"" He goes on to say that from Baghdad to Marrakesh, "there is a common language, common faith, and a common historical and cultural tradition" (Alamney. 1981:13).

Taj Hargey, Director of the Muslim Educational Centre of Oxford in England says, "There is nothing in the Quran that justifies honour killings. There is nothing that says you should kill for the honour of the family. This idea that 'somehow a girl has besmirched our honour and therefore the thing to do is kill her' is bizarre, and Muslims should stop using this defence." He then continued in the article on the MECO website to defend Islam and say that Islam does not approve of honour killings but rather Arabic culture does. Hargey says "the practice is cultural, not religious in origin."

The root of honour killings is centuries old and dates back to the Pre-Islamic era called Jahiliyah (Time of Ignorance before Mohammed). There is a crude old Arab Proverb that says "A man's honour is found between the legs of a women." Originally honour killings were part of the Baluch and Pashtun tribal custom and were founded on the twin concepts of honour and commodification of women. Neshay Najam writing on Honour Killings in Pakistan on the Islamic Awareness Website: "The Pashtoon have codified the honour system in the Pashtoonwali, it revolves around four concepts: 'malmastya', the obligation to show hospitality; 'badal', revenge; 'nanawaty', asylum; and 'nang', honour. A man's property, wealth and all that is linked with these is a sum total of his honour value." This linkage is the point that gives birth to honour killings. If a man's honour is believed to be found between the legs of a woman, it is up to the man to protect his honour by controlling his women. Due to the fact that women were commodified, ie, a daughter's virginity was transferred to a future husband through the payment of a bride price—the spoiling of a woman's purity, through adultery, fornication, rape, or anyone of these rumoured, "a woman loses her inherent value as an object worthy of possession and therefore her right to life. In most tribes, there is no other punishment for a woman accused of 'illicit' sex but death. (Gill 2006: Vol 1 Issue 1 Jan P68).

Irshad Manji, the author of *Allah, Liberty and Love: Courage to Reconcile Faith and Freedom*, said there was another conflict at work in honour killings. It is "a tribal tradition that emphasizes the family or the tribe or the community over the individual" (Manji 2011:63). We in the West just don't have this worldview. Manji being interviewed on CNN went on to say "Although the practice (Honour Killings) may not be Islamic, not all Muslims understand the distinction. It is a problem within Islam because of how Muslims often confuse culture and religion." This seems to be the crux of the problem. Muslims have interpreted Arabic cultural traditions as Islamic when in essence these cultural traditions should be separated out. Manji's final comment to CNN on their Belief Blog Website was "It's Muslims who have to learn to separate culture and religion. If we don't, Islam will continue to get the bad name that it gets"

Indonesia is the world's most populated Muslim nation with 250 million people. Interestingly, Indonesia experiences very little honour killings. Interesting because Indonesia is a non Arabic Muslim nation, thereby adding weight to the argument that honour killings, originating in Arabic tribal culture have found a resting place in skewed Islamic teachings that have become almost a non sanctioned but popularly held Islamic tradition or Hadith. The Australian Refugee Review Tribunal writing on the UNHCR website "Information was found to indicate that honour killings, those that are commonly associated with tribal cultures of the Middle East, rarely occur in Indonesia." This thought was further backed up by Azyumardi Azra, the director of the graduate school at the State Islamic University in Jakarta, Indonesia, quoted on the CNN's Belief Blog website: "No such a practice (Honour Killings) can be found among Indonesian Muslims.

Honour Killings in Europe

A strong case can be made that the concept of honour killings are in fact based in the birth place of European law—Rome. IJaz Ahmad on the website Muslim Debate Initiative, introduces this concept by stating that "Roman society at one point in time functioned on the socio-cultural institution known as *pater familias*, commonly translated as '*father of the family*.' In this tradition, the father is seen as the head of the household, the person with the most authority." With this patriarchal concept in mind we find the first justification for an honor killing in Roman Legalistic Tradition, some 300-400 years before the Prophet Muhammad. Bruce Frier and Thomas McGinn in a *Casebook on Roman Family Law* put this quote forward as they build a case for Honour Killings in Roman Law. "The Emperor Marcus Aurelius and his son Commodus (coreign: A.D. 175–180) sent this rescript: "If a husband, borne on a flood of anger, kills his wife whom he catches in adultery, he will at least not receive the penalty of the lex Cornelia on murderers" (Frier and McGinn 2004:114). The basis for this thought is found in a quote further along that says "When a man does not deny that he killed his wife whom he caught in adultery, capital punishment can be remitted, since it is very hard to restrain legitimate anger" (Frier and McGinn 2004:114.) Very hard to restrain legitimate anger? Men making laws for men who have been cheated on. Making legal opportunity for these cheated men to bring down brutal and swift punishment on the woman who has rejected him. Is this a case of brutal Rome, protecting the bruised egos of their men?

Tom Holmberg, writing on The Napoleon Series website, says that the Roman thought was carried over into French Civil Code, "A man who, in a fit of passion, murdered his spouse *in flagrante delicto* was guilty of no crime. A woman in the same situation was subject to the rigors of the law." Interestingly in the *Journal of Transitional Law and Policy*, Dan Stigall says that the Ottoman Empire tended to blend French and Islamic law, but Egypt, who are very influential across the Islamic world, totally embraced French Law. (Fall Vol 16:1 2006 P9)

Drawing this section to some kind of conclusion, the evidence points to honour killings being centred in Islamic countries based in the Arabic Middle East. These countries not only had honour killings in the culture of their tribal birth place, but they seemingly have skewed Qu'ranic and Hadithic teachings to fit these residual tribal leanings. Additionally, Roman law, passed down through the French conquest of Egypt, provided historical legislation that enshrined in law the killing of adulterous women. To get your head around this: a woman caught in adultery has tribal cultural reasons why she should be killed, religious writings why she should be killed, religious traditions on why she should be killed, and 1000 year old legislation enshrining in law why she should be killed.

A Christian's Missilogical Response

How should Christian's respond to this issue of honour killings? First there needs to be an awareness of the extent of the issue and a broad understanding of the roots of honour killings. For a Christian to humbly understand that seemingly in the Old Testament honour killings were part of the Sinatic Legislation given to the Children of

Israel is also a good starting point. Additionally there needs to be a wide disconnect away from making inflammatory and ignorant comments that stereotype Muslim people as "wife killers" and the like. During the many hours or research and reading that I undertook for this paper, I read some shockingly offensive articles and comments about Muslims and Islam in general, from apparent Christians. In my experience no positive influence happens through causing offense, however the more I understand about Muslim culture, the more pathways are opened up for me to be able to connect and development relationships with my fellow human beings: who are right now, believers in Islam.

Christians can also respond through the petition of Governments and/or involvement in political advocacy groups, to bring about a change in laws that go soft on the perpetrators of family murders. If these murders are part of the cultural context in which a Christian is living, the establishment of shelters for Muslim women and girls, can give a safe place for these women and girls to flee to. Of course if this is not the context that a Christian is living in, such as I find myself in Australia, then the donation of finances to such shelters in Muslim countries is equally effective.

Finally, as Jesus placed great value on women as He walked the earth, we too as Christians can mirror that in a number of ways: How we treat Muslim women when we meet them, the respect we show for them and their culture, being an advocate for women's rights, championing the education of women, particularly Muslim school girls and of course, we can pray for them.

Conclusion

Honour Killings are a tragic response by a family member when another family member strays or apparently strays from the Arabic Islamic cultural norms. With official figures at 5000 women a year being killed and unconfirmed suggestions that the figure is 4 times that, a voice must be given to those who have no voice. This paper is part of that voice. It has traced the roots of honour killings not only back to Pre-Islamic Arabic Culture, but also back through French influenced Egyptian Law, where the French ultimately were influenced by Rome, who legislated that it was ok to kill your adulterous wife. Additionally the fusing together of cultural influences into what is deemed "Islamic" as well as some common interpretations of Islam that devalues and commodifies women mixed into a culture that is Shame/Honour based, has cemented honour killings into Arabic Muslim Culture. Indonesia stands as an example to the rest of the Islamic world, that you can be strictly Muslim and not be involved in honour killings. The key thing here is that Indonesia is not an Arabic nation. So to answer the thesis of this paper:—Are Honour Killings rooted in Islam? The answer is both yes and no. I started this paper with a tale of two wives. But it's also a tale of two religions. It could also be a tale of two testaments—the Old Testament and the New Testament. It's a tale of law and grace. My prayer for Islam is that it will know the grace of the Lord Jesus Christ.

References Cited

Adrian. M. 2011 *A Common Life Amidst Fragmentation: A Consideration of German and French Approaches to the Integration of Muslims.* Journal of Muslim Minority Affairs, Vol. 31, No. 3, September 2011

Ahmad I.. *Honour Killings and Islam.* Muslim Debate Initiative [http://thedebateinitiative.com/2013/06/03/honour-killings-and-islam/>]Last Viewed 13th November 2013.

Almaney. A *Cultural Traits of the Arabs.* Management International Review. Vol 21 No. 3 1981 pp10-18

Author Unknown. *Women Under Islam.* All About Muhammad [http://allaboutmuhammad.com/women-under-islam1.html] Last viewed on the 20th November 2013

Author Unknown. *Ending Violence against Women and Girls*, State of the World Population 2000 New York: United Nations Population Fund, 2000, chap. 3.),

Author Unknown. *Is there any evidence of honour killing in Indonesia?* Australia: Refugee Review Tribunal, *Indonesia: 1.* 21 February

2008, [http://www.refworld.org/docid/4b6fe1f80.html] Last Access 18th November 2013

Author Unknown. *Honour Killings*. Answering Islam [http://www.answering-islam.org/authors/oskar/honor_killings.htm] Last viewed 15th November 2013

Author Unknown. *Women in Islam – Honour Killings*. Questions about Islam. [http://www.questionsaboutislam.com/women-in-islam/islam-honour-killing.php] Last Viewed 10th November 2013

Author Unknown. *Muslim Statistics (Honour Violence)* WikiIslam The Online Resource on Islam [http://wikiislam.net/wiki/Muslim_Statistics_-_Honor_Violence] Last Accessed 23rd November 2013

Burgess, Tina. 2013. *Honour Killing: Father burns 15 years old – daughter to death for talking to fiancé*. Examiner. [http://www.examiner.com/article/honor-killing-father-burns-15-year-old-daughter-to-death-for-talking-to-fiance] Last viewed on the 18th November 2013

Chesler. Phyllis. *World Wide Trends in Honour Killings*. Middle East Quarterly. Spring 2010 pp 3-11

Crilly, Ron *Pakistan Girls Murdered in Honour Killing*. The Telegraph 1st July 2013 [http://news.nationalpost.com/2013/07/01/pakistan-girls-murdered-in-honour-killing-over-video-of-them-dancing-in-the-rain/] Last accessed 18th November 2013

Faqir, Fadia. (2001) '*Intrafamily femicide in defence of honour: the case of Jordan*', Third World Quarterly, Vol 22, no 1: 65-82

Freed, Lisa. Leach, Jonathan. 2012. *Was Noor Almaleki The Victim of an Honour Killing?* CBS News. [http://www.cbsnews.com/8301-18559_162-57408082/was-noor-almaleki-the-victim-of-an-honor-killing/] Last viewed on the 11th November 2013

Frier, Bruce. McGinn, Thomas. 2004 A Casebook on Roman Family Law", Oxford University Press – 2004

Gill. A. International Journal of Criminal Justice Sciences. Patriarchal violence in the name of honor Vol1 Issue 1 Jan 2006

Greene, Richard. *Islam Doesn't Justify Honour Killings Experts Insist*. CNN Belief Blog. [http://religion.blogs.cnn.com/2012/01/30/islam-doesnt-justify-honor-murders-experts-insist/] *Last Viewed 22nd November 2013*

Hargey Taj. *Muslim Education Centre of Oxford 2011 Forum.* Muslim Education Centre of Oxford [http://www.meco.org.uk/] Last viewed on the 21st November 2013

Holmberg Tom. *The Napoleon Series: The Civil Code Index.* The Napoleon Series [http://www.napoleon-series.org/research/government/code/c_code2.html] Last Accessed 17th November 2013

Holy Bible, New Living Translation copyright © 1996, 2004, 2007 by Tyndale House Foundation.

Hosseini, Khaled. 2007. *A thousand Splendid Suns.* NY:Simon and Schuster:

Manar, Hasan. 2002 *The Politics of Honor: Patriarchy, the State and the Murder of Women in the Name of Family Honour.* Journal of Israeli History: Politics, Society, Culture, 21:1-2, 1-37,.

Mallouhi, Christine. 2004. *Miniskirts, Mothers and Muslims.* Oxford:Lion Hudson

Manji I. 2011 *Allah, Liberty and Lover: Courage to Reconcile Faith and Freedom.* Free Press:NY

Mirza, Syed. Honour Killing is Absolutely Islamic. Islam Watch http://www.islam-watch.org/syedkamranmirza/honor_killing.htm *Last Viewed 15th November 2013*

Meeto, Veena. Mirza, Heidi. *Women's Studies,* International Forum Volume 30, Issue 3, May–June 2007, Pages 187–200

Najam, Neshay. *Honour Killings in Pakistan.* Islam Awareness http://www.islamawareness.net/HonourKilling/pakistan.html Last accessed on the 17th November 2013

Nesheiwat, K Ferris. *Honour Crimes in Jordan: Their Treatment Under Islamic and Jordanian Criminal Laws.* Penn State International Law Review. Vol 23:2 P 54 2004

Papas, Voula. *Islam and Women's Rights.* Atheist Foundation http://atheistfoundation.org.au/article/islam-and-womens-rights/ Last Viewed 11th November 2013

Petersen, Freya 2012. *Taliban Publicly Execute Woman Accused of Adultery.* Global Post Afghanistan. [(http://www.globalpost.com/dispatch/news/regions/asia-pacific/afghanistan/120708/taliban-afghanistan-public-execution-adultery)] Last viewed 19th November 2013.

Satkunanandan, Shyamalie. *The Stories Behind Rania's Honour Killings*. Wadi Online [http://en.wadi-online.de/index.php?option=com_content&view=article&id=1039:the-stories-behind-ranias-honor-killings&catid=11:analyse&Itemid=108] *Last viewed 15th November 2013*

Scripture taken from the NEW AMERICAN STANDARD BIBLE®, Copyright © 1960,1962,1963,1968,1971,1972,1973,1975,1977,1995 by The Lockman Foundation.

Tutku, Redjeb. 2013. *Violence against women: Turkey and the economics of honor killings* NY: ST Johns University

Wadud, Amina. 1999 *Qu'ran and Women. Rereading the Sacred Text from a Woman's Perspective.* NY:Oxford University Press

Sexism, Not Religion, Causes Honor Killings

Syarif Hidayat

In the following viewpoint, blogger Syarif Hidayat contends that honor killing arises from cultural, not religious beginnings and most commonly occurs in particularly conservative and patriarchal societies within Muslim communities. As evidence, he cites a most basic tenet in the Quran about an individual's right to life.

As you read, consider the following questions:

1. According to Hidayat, what do Islamic leaders say about the practice of honor killing?
2. According to one piece of evidence cited by the author, why is religion not a causative factor in honor killing?
3. What is *izzat*, and why is it a motivational factor in honor killing?

An **honor killing** or **honour killing** is the homicide of a member of a family or social group by other members, due to the belief of the perpetrators that the victim has brought dishonor upon the family or community. Honor killings are directed mostly against women and girls, but have been extended to men.

The perceived dishonor is normally the result of one of the following behaviors, or the suspicion of such behaviors: dressing in a manner unacceptable to the family or community, wanting to

"'Honor Killing': A Crime Against Islam—In Islam, The Right To Life Is An Absolute Value," by Syarif Hidayat, December 6, 2012. Reprinted by permission.

terminate or prevent an arranged marriage or desiring to marry by own choice, especially if to a member of a social group deemed inappropriate, engaging in heterosexual acts outside marriage and engaging in homosexual acts.

There is a consensus over the fact that crimes of honor emanate from cultural and not religious roots and that they can be found worldwide, mainly in patriarchal societies or communities. However it's also an established fact that they mostly take place within Muslim communities. The paradox is that crimes against women committed in the name of family honor are not sanctioned by Islam and many Islamic leaders have condemned this practice on the grounds that it has no religious basis.

Honor crimes should be contextualized within the larger problem of violence against women in general. Many European women suffer from domestic violence, from crimes that are committed within the conjugal home by the women's spouse or companion. According to a report presented to the Parliamentary Assembly of the Council of Europe on September 16, 2004, domestic violence against women is escalating in Europe and the problem extends to all Council of Europe member states. The report states that domestic violence against women "knows no geographical boundaries, has no age limit, is not the preserve of any particular race, and occurs in every kind of family relationship and in every sort of social milieu."

According to a report titled "So-called honor crimes" presented to the Parliamentary Assembly of the Council of Europe in March 2003, the so-called "honor crimes" occur and affect a whole spectrum of cultures, communities, religions and ethnicities in a wide range of countries around the world including Afghanistan, Bangladesh, Brazil, Egypt, India, Iran, Israel, Jordan, Lebanon, Nigeria, Pakistan, Palestine, Peru, the United States of America, Turkey, the United Kingdom, Italy, Norway, Sweden and Germany.

Also from the same report: Some 5,000 women fall victim to "honor killings" around the world every year.

The United Nations Population Fund (UNFPA) estimates that perhaps as many as 5,000 women and girls a year are killed by members of their own families. Many women's groups in the Middle East and Southwest Asia suspect the number of victims is about four times greater. As noted earlier it is impossible to accurately determine the number of honor killings. Because of shame and threats within the community, witnesses are not willing to speak up and the deaths are usually explained and registered as accidents or suicide. In many countries women are not even aware that a crime has occurred and they may sometimes think that the punishment is deserved.

In the Modern Age, the term "Honor Killing" was First Used in 1978

In the modern age, the term was first used by a Dutch scholar of Turkish society, Ane Nauta in 1978. Nauta sought a term that could be used to distinguish honor killings from blood feuds.

Human Rights Watch defines "honor killings" as follows:

> Honor killings are acts of vengeance, usually death, committed by male family members against female family members, who are held to have brought dishonor upon the family. A woman can be targeted by (individuals within) her family for a variety of reasons, including: refusing to enter into an arranged marriage, being the victim of a sexual assault, seeking a divorce—even from an abusive husband—or (allegedly) committing adultery. The mere perception that a woman has behaved in a way that "dishonors" her family is sufficient to trigger an attack on her life.

Some women who bridge social divides, publicly engage other communities, or adopt some of the customs or the religion of an outside group may be attacked. In countries that receive immigration, some otherwise low-status immigrant men and boys have asserted their dominant patriarchal status by inflicting honor killings on women family members who have participated in public life, for example in feminist and integration politics.

Men can also be the victims of honor killings by members of the family of a woman with whom they are perceived to have an inappropriate relationship

Cultural implications can often be seen in public and private views of honor killings. In some cultures, honor killings are considered less serious than pre-meditated murders simply because they arise from long-standing cultural traditions and are thus deemed appropriate or justifiable. Additionally, according to a poll done by the BBC's Asian network, 1 in 10 of the 500 Hindus, Sikhs, Christians and Muslim surveyed, said they would condone any murder of someone who threatened their family's honor. The poll demonstrated how the notion of honor killings and views of whether they are acceptable and justifiable crosses religion and is more contingent on the family's social culture.

Islam is Against the Killing—in Islam, the Right to Life Is an Absolute Value

Tahira Shaid Khan, a professor of women's issues at Aga Khan University, notes that there is nothing in Al Qur'an that permits or sanctions honor killings. The first and most basic right in the Qur'an that every Muslim is expected to follow is, in fact, the right to life. As written in the Qur'an.

> In the Name of Allah, the Beneficent, the Merciful. *"Because of that We ordained for the Children of Israel that if anyone killed a person not in retaliation (in legal punishment) of murder, or (and) to spread mischief in the land—it would be as if he killed all mankind, and if anyone saved a life, it would be as if he saved the life of all mankind. And indeed, there came to them Our Messengers with clear proofs, evidence, and signs, even then after that many of them continued to exceed the limits (e.g. by doing oppression unjustly and exceeding beyond the limits set by Allâh by committing the major sins) in the land!"*—Al Qur'an, Surah Al-Maidah, Verse 32.

Professor Khan instead blames it on attitudes (across different classes, ethnic and religious groups) that view women as property with no rights of their own as the motivation for honor killings. Khan also argues that this view results in violence against women and their being turned "into a commodity which can be exchanged, bought and sold."

Widney Brown, the advocacy director of Human Rights Watch, said that the practice "goes across cultures and across religions." Human rights advocates have compared "honor killing" to "crimes of passion" in Latin America (which are sometimes treated extremely leniently) and also to the killing of women for lack of dowry in India.

Representatives of Islamist pressure groups including Council on American-Islamic Relations (CAIR) and the Canadian Islamic Congress, various academics (e.g., Ajay Nair, Tom Keil), activists (e.g., Rana Husseini), and religious leaders (e.g., Abdulhai Patel of the Canadian Council of Imams) have insisted that honor killings either do not exist or have nothing to do with Islam; that they are cultural, tribal, pre-Islamic customs, and that, in any event, domestic violence exists everywhere.

Western Feminists who work with the victims of domestic violence in the western countries have seen so much violence against women that they are uncomfortable singling out one group of perpetrators, especially an immigrant or Muslim group. However, Western domestic femicide differs significantly from honor killing.

No Definite Connection with Religion at All

According to Dr. Shahrzad Mojab, a University of Toronto professor of women's studies, followers of Hinduism, Islam, Judaism and Christianity have used their religions as a rationale to commit honor killings. However, Mojab stated that honor killings don't have "any definite connection with religion at all." She also pointed out that honor killings have been practiced before any major religion came into existence.

Here are the analysis, observation and comments about "Honor Killings" from the Muslim Council of Britain (MCB). The recent tragic murders of two young British Muslim women have once again focused media and public attention on the subject of honor killings. The MCB office has received a steady stream of media enquiries seeking clarification on the stance of Islam on this subject. We have made it very clear to reporters and would like to take this opportunity to re-state that honor killings are in no way, shape or form condoned by Islam. On the contrary, Islam categorically denounces vigilantism, rather encouraging mercy, justice and the rule of law.

> *The Merciful (Allah SWT) is kind to those who are merciful. If you show compassion to your fellow creatures in this world, then those in heaven shall be compassionate toward you.*—The Prophet MuhammadPBUH, as narrated by Abd'Allah bin Amr.

That said, it would be naive of us to bury our heads in the sand and deny that this pre-Islamic custom continues amongst some Muslims and those of other faith communities (Scotland Yard have gone on record to say that there were an estimated 12 "honor killings" in the UK last year stating that these were not restricted to Muslims, but also occurred in Sikh and Christian families). For our part, we must acknowledge that this is a problem, which is found within a very small section of the British Muslim community. We at the MCB hope to work with specialists in this area to try to address this problem and the underlying issues and, God Willing, in due course to reduce the incidence of honor killing.

Why then do such tragic events occur? Let us consider the example of the Muslim man recently given a life sentence for slitting his daughter's throat in an "Honor Killing" after she began dating a Christian. This is a tragic story of irreconcilable cultural differences between a father who had a traditional "Muslim" upbringing, values and background and a daughter who had adopted non-Islamic cultural life.

But a devout Muslim who understands their religion correctly would certainly never take another life. In reality, such tragedies have nothing to do with true faith. Her father's sense of shame at his daughter's actions led to him taking her life in the erroneous belief that this act would redeem the family name. The concept of respect or *izzat* is a very strong motivating factor amongst non-Caucasian races, regardless of their religious affiliation. Its origins appear to stem from tribal, clan or village origins. This is in sharp contradistinction to the teachings of our noble religion Islam, in which it is held that all individuals are personally responsible for their own actions. Her father's un-Islamic action is liable for punishment under Islamic law.

This practice of "honor killing" is a form of murder without trial, which is contrary to Islam. Islam upholds the sanctity of human life, as the Holy Qur'an declares that *killing one innocent human being is akin to killing the entire human race* (Qur'an 5:32, 6:151, 17:33). Like all other faith traditions, Islam considers all forms of life as sacred. There is certainly no justification for such a practice of "Honor Killing" in Islamic Law (Shariah). It is pertinent here to consider this issue in more detail.

The Equality of Women and Men before Allah SWT

Islam considers a woman to be equal to a man as a human being and as his partner in this life. Women have been created with a soul of the same nature as man's. Allah (SWT) says in the Holy Qur'an:

> "O mankind! Be dutiful to your Lord, Who created you from a single person (Adam), and from him (Adam) He created his wife (Eve), and from them both He created many men and women and fear Allah through Whom you demand your mutual (rights), and (do not cut the relations of) the wombs (kinship). Surely, Allah is Ever and All-Watcher over you." (Al-Nisa 4:1)

And in the words of the Prophet Muhammad (SAW): *"Assuredly, women are the twin halves of men."* (Sahih reported by Abu-Dawud (RA)

Islam recognizes and celebrates the inherent dignity bestowed by God (Allah SWT) upon all human beings regardless of race, ethnicity, gender or religion. The Qur'an is explicit in its emphasis on the equality of women and men before God:

"And their Lord has accepted of them and answered them, "Never will I suffer to be lost the work of any of you, whether male or female, you are members, one of another..." (3:195; see also 33:35)

Individual accountability before God is stressed throughout the Qur'an, beginning with the story of Adam and Eve: as a result of their transgression (committed together and simultaneously) they were banished from Paradise and made to toil on Earth. God chose to forgive them both and so their sin is not inherited by subsequent generations. Similarly, as exemplified in the following verse:

"Whoever chooses to follow the right path follows it but for his own good; and whoever goes astray, goes but astray to his own hurt; and no bearer of burdens shall be made to bear another's burden." (17:15)

It is clear that one individual, no matter how guilty, cannot transfer that guilt to another. So for a woman who does engage in illicit sexual activity (Zina), she and she alone bears the consequences as determined by God.

The problem of "honor killings" is not a problem of morality or of ensuring that women maintain their own personal virtue; rather, it is a problem of domination, power and hatred of women who, in these instances, are viewed as nothing more than servants to the family, both physically and symbolically.

And the sad consequences of this domination are that thousands of girls and women across the globe (although mostly centered in the Middle East) are murdered by male family members each year in the name of family honor. Honor killings are executed for instances of rape, infidelity, flirting or any other instance perceived as disgracing the family's honor, and the woman is then killed by a male relative to restore the family's name in the community. Many women are killed based on suspicions of a family member and are not given the chance to defend themselves. The allegation alone is enough to defile a man's or family's honor and is therefore enough to justify the killing of the woman. The men who commit the murder typically go unpunished or receive reduced sentences.

Honor Killing is Actually a pre-Islamic, Tribal Custom

Honor killings tend to be prevalent in countries with a majority Muslim population, but many Islamic leaders and scholars condemn the practice and deny that it is based on religious doctrine. Honor killing is actually a pre-Islamic, tribal custom stemming from the patriarchal and patrilineal society's interest in keeping strict control over familial power structures.

Because these crimes often go unreported, it is difficult to determine the actual number of victims in honor killings. The United Nations Population Fund estimates as many as 5000 females being killed each year.

Islam is clear on its prohibition of sexual relationships outside of marriage. This prohibition does not distinguish between men and women, even though, in some countries, women are uniformly singled out for punishment of sexual crimes while the men, even rapists, may be treated with impunity. In order for a case to even be brought before a Muslim court, several strict criteria must be met. The most important is that any accusation of illicit sexual behavior must have been seen by four witnesses; and they must have been witness to the act of sexual intercourse itself. Other forms of intimacy do not constitute zina and therefore are not subject to any legal consequences even though they are not appropriate and are considered sinful.

On the other hand, a woman falsely accused of zina has in her support the Qur'an, which spells out harsh consequences for those accusers who are unable to support their allegations with four witnesses. The Prophet Muhammad (peace and blessing of God be upon him) was known for his clemency, even if the accusations met the criteria, for he recognized the seriousness of the matter. In addition, there is no evidence whatsoever that he condoned any form of retribution that singled out women and he was swift to ensure that those accused of any crime received due process to guarantee justice. It is important to know that all innocent lives are equal in Islam.

There is no difference between the rich and the poor, the man and the woman, the free and the slave. All are equal in the eyes of God:

> *"...if any one slew a person -unless it be for murder or for spreading mischief in the land -it would be as if he slew the whole people: and if any one saved a life, it would be as if he saved the life of the whole people...*(The Qur'an 5:32)"

From the above Noble Verses, we see that if you kill one innocent soul (whether it was a Muslim soul or not), then it is like committing a crime against all people. We also see that God Almighty considers the innocent soul as a "sacred" soul.

The Distortion of Islam

Unfortunately, the legal safeguards to protect women and men from indiscriminate and unlawful enforcement of presumed Islamic injunctions have been forgotten Indeed, the legal system and law enforcement agencies including police officers and prison guards, have been implicated in the perpetuation of the problem by their willful lenience towards men who have carried out an assault in the name of "honor" and by their abuse and denigration of women who stand accused.

Muslims today must unequivocally reject this distortion of Islam that is used to violate the most basic Islamic rights of human decency, integrity and justice. Unwillingness on the part of the Muslim community to address these issues in a forthright and unapologetic manner is borne out of an inherent distrust of perceived "Western" attempts to taint the image of Islam in the interest of global politics. This is no excuse for us to turn a blind eye to injustices committed against Muslims and others, especially when the perpetrators are members of the same faith.

Confronting the problem of "honor killings" and other crimes that disproportionately affect women requires a change in attitude that pervades all levels of society where such attacks occur. Muslim leaders can provide an important example to their followers by taking an unequivocal stand against behavior that is in direct violation of Islam. Attempts must be made to change the socio-cultural beliefs that underpin honor killings. Concomitant attention must be paid to meeting basic socioeconomic needs and solving problems stemming from deprivation, unemployment and poor education that are often at the root of disturbing social trends that seek out the most disenfranchised to serve as scapegoats.

> "O you who believe! Stand out firmly for justice, as witnesses to God, even as against yourselves, or your parents, or your kin, and whether it be (against) rich or poor: For God can best protect both. Follow not the lusts (of your hearts), lest you swerve, and if you distort (justice) or decline to do justice, verily God is well-acquainted with all that you do." (Qur'an 4:135)

We must combat the woeful disrespect for human life in a variety of ways. We have to change some cultural and societal perceptions of the place and value of women in our society according to the Islamic value system. We must commit ourselves to a multi-faceted approach to changing the minds, and hearts of those who limit women's potential or their worth and status in our society. Islamic true values must be upheld at all cost. The practice of honor killing must be condemned and the true teaching of Islam must be upheld. (Source: The Muslim Council of Britain).

Honor Killings in the Bible

Many Christians are often fond of accusing Muslims of committing several honor killings in the name of Islam; they then use this line of argument as a reason to discredit Islam in their eyes. In this article we shall once again turn the table on the Christian showing that honor killings can be found in the Bible, and that the Bible is for honor killings! Hence by their own criteria, Christians will have to abandon their own book.

Let us now see the honor killings in the Bible:

Lev 21:9 And the daughter of any priest, if she profane herself by playing the whore, she profaneth her father: she shall be burnt with fire.

So note, if the priest's daughter commits a bad sexual act, she is to be burned because of her father's reputation, because it is against his honor. What will the Christian say now? This is one example of honor killing in the Bible, in fact the act is ordered by the Bible itself.

"And he that curseth his father, or his mother, shall surely be put to death. (Exodus 21:17)"

"For every one that curseth his father or his mother shall be surely put to death: he hath cursed his father or his mother; his blood shall be upon him. (Leviticus 20:9)"

So here the children are put to death for insulting their parents, this is another example of honor killings, the children are put to death for dis-honoring their very own parents and the punishment is death.

So we have seen 3 examples of honor killings in the Bible, so since Christians always have a problem with honor killings and say Islam is wrong because of some Muslims who commit this act, then the Bible is also wrong for allowing honor killings which also makes their own God wrong, and if God is wrong then he cant be God because God is always correct. Either way the Christian is in a bad dilemma.

What Must Be Done

"Honor" killing is a global phenomenon. To combat the epidemic of honor killings requires understanding what makes these murders unique. They differ from plain and psychopathic homicides, serial killings, crimes of passion, revenge killings, and domestic violence. Their motivation is different and based on codes of morality and behavior that typify some cultures, often reinforced by fundamentalist religious dictates. In 2000, the United Nations estimated that there are 5,000 honor killings every year. In 2002 and again in 2004, the U.N. brought a resolution to end honor killings and other honor-related crimes.

How can this problem be addressed? Law enforcement agencies and religious authorities must all be included in education, prevention, and prosecution efforts in the matter of honor killings.

In addition, shelters for battered girls and women should be established and multilingual staff appropriately trained in the facts about honor killings. For example, young Muslim girls are frequently lured back home by their mothers. When a shelter resident receives such a phone call, the staff must immediately go on high alert. The equivalent of a federal witness protection program for the intended targets of honor killings should be created; England has already established such a program. Extended safe surrogate family networks must be created to replace existing family networks; the intended victims themselves, with enormous assistance, may become each other's "sisters."

The government in each country should adopt appropriate legislative, legal and financial measures in order to prevent and punish honor killings and to assist the victims. However, much more importantly, what is needed is a change in consciousness and it can only be achieved through education on the one hand and economic development on the other. (HSH)

Bibliotheque:

MCB Direct position statement on Honor Killings http://www.mcb.org.uk

Muslim Women's League, USA Position Paper on Honor Killings

http://www.meforum.org/2646/worldwide-trends-in-honor-killings

http://www.turkishculture.org/lifestyles/turkish-culture-portal/the-women/honor-killings-426.htm

"Honor Killings in the Bible" written by Sami Zaatari

http://muslim-responses.com/Honor_Killings/Honor_Killings_

http://www.jihadwatch.org/2009/12/uk-honor-crimes-up-40-due-to-rising-christian-fundamentalism—-no-wait.html

http://www.dailymail.co.uk/news/article-1233918/Honour-crime-40-rising-fundamentalism.html

http://en.wikipedia.org/wiki/Honor_killing#Europe

http://timesofindia.indiatimes.com/india/Honour-killing-Its-a-global-phenomenon/articleshow/6154172.cms?intenttarget=no

Periodical and Internet Sources Bibliography

The following articles have been selected to supplement the diverse views presented in this chapter.

Fred Barbash. "'She wouldn't listen': A wrenching story of an 'honor killing' in Pakistan," *Washington Post*, October 5, 2016.

James Emery. "Reputation is Everything," *World & I,* vol. 18, issue 5, May 2003, pp. 182.

Luis Granados. "Saving Aqsa Parvez," *Humanist,* vol. 70, issue 5, September-October 2010, pp. 18-21.

Arsalan Iftikhar. "Honor Killings Are A Global Problem," *Time,* July 29, 2016. http://time.com/4415554/honor-killing-qandeel-baloch/.

Ziauddin Sardar. "Forced marriages disgrace Islam," *New Statesman,* vol. 137, issue 4890, March 31, 2008, pp. 23.

Steph Solis. "Pakistani woman burns daughter alive for eloping," *USA Today,* June 9, 2016. http://www.usatoday.com/story/news/world/2016/06/09/pakistan-mother-burns-daughter/85635530/.

Robert Spencer. "Honor Killings Tolerated by Islamic Teachings," *Human Events,* vol. 66, issue 24, July 5, 2010.

Robert Spencer. "Jihad Watch," *Human Events,* vol. 65, issue 9, March 2, 2009, pp. 17.

GLOBALVIEWPOINTS

CHAPTER 3

Violence Against Women is on the Rise Worldwide

In the United States, Honor Killing Is More Common Than You Think

Robert Spencer

In the following viewpoint, Jihad Watch director Robert Spencer asserts that, according to the Department of Justice, there is a mounting number of honor killings in the United States—and Spencer claims that Islamic law encourages this violence. He cites statistical evidence from a DOJ research study that estimates the number of honor killings in the United States to be about twenty-three to twenty-seven per year and insists that the unreported killings number even higher.

As you read, consider the following questions:

1. According to statistics reported by Spencer, what percentage of worldwide honor killings are committed by Muslims?
2. What is the reason behind a large number of honor killings in the United States cited by the author?
3. As reported by Spencer, what will cause honor-based violence to continue to worsen?

E ven cases that appear to be honor killings, such as the Jan. 1, 2008 murder of two Irving, Texas, sisters that landed their father on the FBI's most wanted list, cannot always be conclusively

"23–27 documented honor killings every year in the U.S., many more go unreported," by Robert Spencer, Jihad Watch, November 10, 2015. Reprinted by permission.

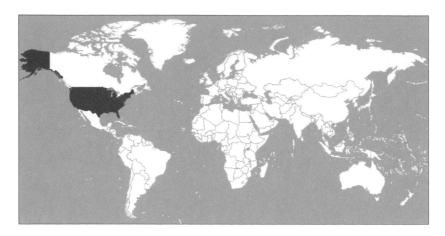

linked to a religious motivation. Without hard evidence, critics say, ascribing a religious motivation to crimes committed by Muslims demeans Islam."

Yaser Said murdered his daughters because they had non-Muslim boyfriends. But to note that fact "demeans Islam," so it must not be said. It no doubt also "demeans Islam" to take any notice of these inconvenient facts:

Muslims commit 91 percent of honor killings worldwide. A manual of Islamic law certified as a reliable guide to Sunni orthodoxy by Al-Azhar University, the most respected authority in Sunni Islam, says that "retaliation is obligatory against anyone who kills a human being purely intentionally and without right." However, "not subject to retaliation" is "a father or mother (or their fathers or mothers) for killing their offspring, or offspring's offspring." ('Umdat al-Salik o1.1-2). In other words, someone who kills his child incurs no legal penalty under Islamic law. In this case, of course, the victim was the murderer's wife, a victim to the culture of violence and intimidation that such laws help create.

The Palestinian Authority gives pardons or suspended sentences for honor murders. Iraqi women have asked for tougher sentences for Islamic honor murderers, who get off lightly now. Syria in 2009 scrapped a law limiting the length of sentences for honor killings, but "the new law says a man can still benefit from extenuating circumstances in crimes of passion or honour 'provided he serves a prison term of no less than two years in the case of killing.'" And in 2003 the Jordanian Parliament voted down on Islamic grounds a provision designed to stiffen penalties for honor killings. Al-Jazeera reported that "Islamists and conservatives said the laws violated religious traditions and would destroy families and values."

Until the encouragement Islamic law gives to honor killing is acknowledged and confronted, more women will suffer.

"Honor killing in America: DOJ report says growing problem is hidden in stats," by Hollie McKay, Fox News, November 10, 2015: The estimated 27 victims of so-called "honor killings" each year in the U.S. don't fit neatly into the FBI's exhaustive Uniform Crime Reporting Statistics.

Hidden among thousands of nondescript murders and cases labeled as domestic violence are a mounting number of killings motivated by a radical and dark interpretation of Islam. Honor killings and violence, which typically see men victimize wives and daughters because of behavior that has somehow insulted their faith, are among the most secretive crimes in society, say experts.

"Cases of honor killings and/or violence in the U.S. are often unreported because of the shame it can cause to the victim and the victim's family," Farhana Qazi, a former U.S. government analyst and senior fellow at the Center for Advanced Studies on Terrorism, told FoxNews.com. "Also, because victims are often young women, they may feel that reporting the crime to authorities will draw too much attention to the family committing the crime."

Even cases that appear to be honor killings, such as the Jan. 1, 2008 murder of two Irving, Texas, sisters that landed their father on the FBI's most wanted list, cannot always be conclusively linked to a religious motivation. Without hard evidence, critics say, ascribing a religious motivation to crimes committed by Muslims demeans Islam. Yet, federal authorities believe they must be able to identify "honor" as a motive for violence and even murder if they are to address a growing cultural problem.

"Honor Violence Measurement Methods," a study released earlier this year by research corporation Westat, and commissioned by the U.S. Department of Justice, identified four types of honor violence: forced marriage, honor-based domestic violence, honor killing and female genital mutilation. The report, which estimated that 23-27 honor killings per year occur in the U.S., noted that 91 percent of victims in North America are murdered for being "too Westernized," and in incidents involving daughters 18 years or younger, a father is almost always involved. And for every honor killing, there are many more instances of physical and emotional abuse, all in the name of fundamentalist Islam, say experts....

In 2012, the mother, father and sister of 19-year-old Aiya Altameemi were charged with beating her because she refused an arranged marriage to an older man.

For police who encounter apparent honor crimes, the investigation is typically treated as a regular crime or murder probe, usually under the umbrella of domestic violence. While both issues are tragic and problematic, experts say there are critical distinctions, and that honor violence requires a different approach.

Detective Chris Boughey, of Peoria, Ariz., calls Oct. 20, 2009, a day that "changed my life forever." That was the day Iraqi immigrant Faleh Almaleki murdered his daughter, Noor Almaleki, by running her over with his vehicle for becoming "too Westernized." Boughey was assigned as the lead investigator and has since dedicated his career to educating others and taking on similar cases in numerous other states—from Alaska and New York to California, Washington state and Pennsylvania.

"In the Almaleki case, I learned very quickly that we would receive no assistance from the family," Boughey said. "In fact, we received out-and-out defiance and resistance. Although we know they are involved, it can be very hard to prove in a court of law."

Other honor-motivated tragedies in the U.S. have garnered headlines.

- In 2012, police arrested the mother, father and sister of 19-year-old Aiya Altameemi in Phoenix after they allegedly beat, restrained and burned her for reportedly declining an arranged marriage with an older man and talking to another boy.

- In 2009, Aasiya Hassan was beheaded by her husband, Muzzammil Hassan, at the Buffalo, N.Y., Muslim TV station where they worked for allegedly requesting a divorce. The Pakistani-born killer defended himself at trial, never denied his guilt and was convicted in 2011. A few months before Hassan was killed, Sandeela Kanwal was strangled by her father outside Atlanta for failing to "be true to her religion" because she wanted to leave an arranged marriage.

- In the 2008 case in Irving, Yasser Said, a cab driver from Egypt, is suspected of shooting his two daughters, Amina, 18, and Sarah Said, 17, in the back of his taxi because they were dating non-Muslim boys and embracing Western culture. Said has been a fugitive ever since....

- And in one of the earliest widely reported cases of honor killing in the U.S., 16-year-old Palestina Isa, of St. Louis, was murdered in 1989 by her father Zein Isa, who was helped by her mother. Zein Isa was angry that his daughter had gotten a job and was dating an African-American boy. Both parents were convicted of murder and sentenced to death. Zein Isa died on death row in 1997, while his wife's sentence was commuted to life in prison without parole.

Honor violence is an even bigger problem in other parts of the Western world, with a reported 11,000 cases of honor violence recorded in the United Kingdom in the last five years while incidents also have been documented in Canada, Germany, France and Sweden.

Baric affirmed that given immigration trends in the last decade —an influx from Middle Eastern and South Asian countries where honor violence is part of the culture—the problem will continue to worsen if authorities don't identify and address it. Boughey said honor violence, whether it be abuse and murder, FGM, or

Honor-Based Violence is a Worldwide Problem

Rabia Bibi, in Pakistan, suffered 70% burns after her father and uncle threw acid on her. They objected to her choice of husband, her cousin Jaffar, with whom she eloped after divorcing her first husband, another cousin, Nazakat.

Although a local council of village elders (panchayat) approved the match, her family did not agree. They attempted to blame the murder on Jaffar, but a police investigation revealed the culprits.

Honor killings are rampant in several cultures. On August 19, in neighboring India, in Uttar Pradesh, a 17-year old girl was beheaded by her brothers who paraded her head around for half an hour.

"This is a lesson to girls who have relationships," they are said to have shouted. "We do not allow our daughters or sisters to have affairs."

In Egypt, a high-school student strangled his sister to death in the rural village of Markaz abu Qaraqas in Al-Minya province last week.

The security chief of Al-Minya, Major-General Hussein Sayyif, received a message from the police chief in Markaz abu Qaraqas, saying the student killed his sister because she became pregnant out of wedlock.

The security forces managed to arrest the accused, identified only as M. Z. aged 17. The investigation is ongoing.

So far this year an estimated seven Arab women in Israel were murdered in honor killings in Israel.

Honor culture and strictly patriarchal societal norms see the reputation of families as vested in the perceived or actual sexual purity of women in these cultures.

In 2000, the U.N. estimated there were 5,000 honor killings per year. Other estimates made by campaigners suggest there may be as many as 20,000 annually.

Despite international campaigns against the practice, it remains widespread.

- *"Spate of Killings Shows Honor Violence is a Worldwide Problem," by Elliot Friedland, Clarion Project, Inc., August 30, 2015.*

forced marriage—is much more widespread in America than most people realize and, as it stands, authorities have no proper system in place to track it....

One of the biggest challenges, Boughey said, is the social pressures to not be deemed "culturally insensitive." That can keep social service agencies from alerting law enforcement when honor violence crosses their radar.

"Some agencies won't intervene even after these young women have come forward," he said. "I am not quite sure when we as a country decided that it was more important to be politically correct than doing the right thing."...

Mainstream Muslims condemn honor violence without equivocation, said Ibrahim Hooper, spokesman for the [Hamas-linked—ed.] Council on American-Islamic Relations (CAIR).

"If anyone mistreats women, they should not seek refuge in Islam," he said.

Republican Muslim Coalition Executive Director Saba Ahmed also said such "barbaric acts" are in total conflict with the teachings of Islam.

In Mexico, Women Look to the Past to End Future Violence

Laurie Liles

In this viewpoint, journalism student Laurie Liles discusses the problem of domestic violence and femicide in Chiapas, Mexico. As part of the Cronkite Borderlands Project, Liles studies specific cases of intimate partner violence, the history of women's rights in Mexico, what part male oppression plays in the prevalence of violence, and the prognosis for the future of women in indigenous communities.

As you read, consider the following questions:

1. What kind of threats do indigenous women in Mexico face?
2. What was different about how women were treated under the Zapatistas and how did that change?
3. Do you think the Women's Revolutionary Law would work in other countries?

S AN CRISTÓBAL DE LAS CASAS, Mexico—When a pending downpour forced Lesvia Entzin Gomez to return to her mother-in-law's without the apples she had left to cut, her drunken, enraged husband pulled out a shotgun.

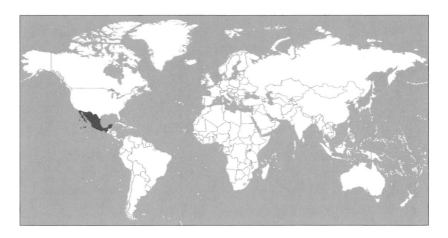

"I did not think he had a shell in the shotgun," Entzin Gomez recalled. "I thought he was playing … then he pointed it at me and I heard it go off. He shot me in the face and my eyes."

The July 15, 2013, attack left the 24-year-old mother of three blind and suffering from headaches and dizziness. Her husband, Jorge Navarro Hernandez, remains in jail, but she said she has been threatened by his relatives and is in constant fear for her life.

Her case is not unusual: 30 percent of women in Chiapas state age 15 and older were victims of domestic violence in 2011, according to Mexico's most-recent National Survey on the Dynamics of Relationships in the Household.

And while that seems shockingly high, Chiapas actually has the lowest domestic violence rate among Mexico's 31 states and federal district. The state of Mexico was highest at 56.9 percent. Nationally, 46.1 percent of Mexico's 42.6 million women reported physical, emotional or psychological abuse in the 2011 survey.

In Chiapas, where more than 70 percent live in poverty, activists say gender-based violence resulted in the deaths of 84 women from January to October 2013. Entzin Gomez narrowly missed becoming one of those statistics.

Telling Her Story

She told her story at a news conference nearly eight months after she was shot. Entzin Gomez kept her eyes downcast and her face partially shrouded beneath a gray woven shawl. Her scars were still visible and she moved slowly with the aid of a companion.

She was flanked by two members of Mexico President Enrique Peña Nieto's Executive Commission for Victims, who said they planned to take Entzin Gomez to Mexico City for medical treatment. But Entzin Gomez said she needed food and a safe place to live with her children.

"Right now we are suffering. We are eating just a little beans and corn," she said.

State and local officials have failed Entzin Gomez and her family, said Dr. Julio Barros Hernandez, one of the commissioners at the news conference.

"In this case, they have left Lesvia totally defenseless, depriving her of the essential rights that allow one to live with dignity," he said.

The other commissioner, Jaime del Rincon Rochin, said her plight is all too common.

"Lesvia is a painful example of the state in which many women are left when they survive an attack of femicide," del Rincon Rochin said. "What Lesvia is living through today is what many women live through in many parts of this country, and we cannot permit that this keeps happening."

Femicide—the act of killing a woman because of her gender—is a federal offense in Mexico, punishable by 40 to 60 years in prison, according to the U.S. State Department's Mexico 2013 Human Rights Report.

Twenty-eight states, including Chiapas and the federal district, have criminalized femicide and domestic abuse, but problems persist.

According to a 2012 report published by the Mexico Secretary of Governance, the number of female homicide victims increased dramatically over the previous three years, particularly in the federal district and eight states, including Chiapas.

And domestic abuse rates may be understated. Domestic violence victims from rural and indigenous communities often do not report abuse, said the State Department report, for fear of reprisal, of the stigma associated with domestic violence or because they may belong to communities where abuse is accepted.

As a result, the report said no authoritative government statistics are available on the number of abusers prosecuted, convicted or punished.

In Chiapas, the fight against domestic violence and for equal treatment has been going on longer than in most states in Mexico.

A Revolutionary Notion

When indigenous rebels known as the EZLN—the Zapatistas—rebelled against the Mexican government on Jan. 1, 1994, the leftist group unveiled a Women's Revolutionary Law as a key feature of their manifesto, the First Declaration of the Lacandon Jungle. It's essentially a 10-article bill of rights for indigenous women.

The articles declare that women have a right to participate in the political system and hold leadership posts; to decide whom to marry and how many children to bear; to a fair wage and quality health care; and to a life free from sexual and domestic violence.

Author and researcher Hilary Klein said that to appreciate what has changed since the Zapatista rebellion you must first understand how cruel life was for indigenous women 30 years ago.

"Women lived in extremely oppressive situations where, in the public sphere and the private sphere, there was an extraordinary level of domestic violence and alcohol abuse," said Klein, who lived and worked with Zapatista women from 1997 to 2003.

Klein's book, *Compañeras: Zapatista Women's Stories,* slated for release in January, documents what she calls the "seismic" transformation women in Zapatista territory experienced before, during and after the 1994 EZLN uprising.

Before the Zapatistas, Klein said, women had no control over their lives.

"They basically had to ask their husbands or their fathers for permission to leave the house," she said. "They were married very young and had children throughout their reproductive years."

As the Zapatistas began to mobilize in the 1980s, Roman Catholic Church leaders inspired by liberation theology influenced the movement, Klein said. Bishop Samuel Ruiz Garcia of the Diocese of San Cristobal de las Casas urged better treatment of women as he helped organize indigenous communities.

"As these leaders were saying, 'It's not OK for women to be treated this way,' there was a simultaneous push from the women themselves, who said they wanted things to change," Klein said.

She said the Zapatistas emphasized women's involvement as a way to grow their movement. EZLN leaders "pushed from the beginning that women can participate at all levels of the organization, and that has been their driving strategy to make changes around women's rights," Klein said.

The Zapatista attack on San Cristóbal de las Casas in 1994 was planned and led by Comandanta Ana Maria. Nearly 30 percent of insurgents were women, and Comandanta Ramona was the sole Zapatista representative at the First National Indian Congress in Mexico City in 1995.

In the years leading up to the rebellion, EZLN activist Susana traveled to dozens of villages throughout Chiapas, collecting suggestions from thousands of indigenous women, according to Klein and other Zapatista historians. Their ideas were ultimately incorporated into the Women's Revolutionary Law.

"No event has been more important for the women's movement in Chiapas than the public appearance of the EZLN in 1994," author and Professor R. Aida Hernandez Castillo wrote in "Contemporary Women's Movements in Chiapas." Hernandez Castillo said the Zapatista movement and the Women's Revolutionary Law were catalysts, prompting indigenous women throughout Mexico to organize.

Zapatista Army of National Liberation Women's Revolutionary Law

First: Women, regardless of their race, creed, color or political affiliation, have the right to participate in the revolutionary struggle in a way determined by their desire and capacity.

Second: Women have the right to work and receive a just salary.

Third: Women have the right to decide the number of children they will have and

Fourth: Women have the right to participate in the affairs of the community and hold positions of authority if they are freely and democratically elected.

Fifth: Women and their children have the right to primary attention in matters of health and nutrition.

Sixth: Women have the right to an education.

Seventh: Women have the right to choose their partner, and are not to be forced

Eighth: Women shall not be beaten or physically mistreated by their family members or by strangers. Rape and attempted rape will be severely punished.

Ninth: Women will be able to occupy positions of leadership in the organization and hold military ranks in the revolutionary armed forces.

Tenth: Women will have all the rights and obligations elaborated in the Revolutionary Laws and regulations.

Source: Rodriguez, Victoria. Women's Participation in Mexican Political Life. Boulder, CO: Westview Press, 1998.

The Movement Stalls

But Klein and local women's leaders say the explosive period of female empowerment of the 1990s has plateaued in recent years.

Human-rights activists' frustration was evident March 8 at an International Women's Day news conference and protest rally that drew about 200 near the base of the large Mayan cross facing the Cathedral of San Cristóbal de Las Casas.

Organizers said the federal and state governments have failed to protect Chiapas women from domestic violence and femicide.

"Violence in Chiapas is extreme," said Center for Women's Rights leader Alma Padilla Garcia in an interview. "All forms of violence, poverty, hunger, all can be considered violence against women. We give responsibility for this violence to the state of Mexico."

Federal and state officials in December launched a domestic-violence prevention program that Chiapas Attorney General Raciel Lopez Salazar says has reduced the number of femicides and crimes committed against women.

In a March 8 statement, the attorney general's office announced a 78 percent decrease in femicide during the first quarter of 2014 compared with the same period in 2013, from nine cases to two. It attributed the reduction to a new program, the Emerging Action Plan for the Prevention and Treatment of Femicide and Gender Violence. The office also said crimes against women declined by 58 percent during the same period.

Coordinated by Mexico's Secretary of Governance, the Ministry for Development and Empowerment of Women and the Chiapas attorney general's office, the initiative includes domestic-violence prevention workshops, media education, law-enforcement training and a 24-hour, toll-free domestic-abuse hotline.

Despite such initiatives, human-rights leaders say complex economic and social challenges continue to thwart progress and threaten women's safety.

Longtime women's rights activist Mercedes Bustamante Olivera, a founder of the Center for Research and Action for Latin Women, said women in Chiapas suffer under a "structure of violence" and male oppression.

"Because the capitalist system is organized on the basis of male parameters," she said, "men are aggressive toward women."

Discrimination against women leads to violence in family and personal relationships that leave women defenseless, Bustamante Olivera said. In order for change to occur, she said women must lead.

"Far from being victims, we take action," she said.

Women Lead the Fight

A growing number of indigenous women in Chiapas are taking action. Pascuala Perez Gutierrez and Margarita Vasquez Boloma work with the Fray Pedro de la Nada Committee for Human Rights, an organization founded shortly after the 1994 uprising to train indigenous people about their fundamental rights.

Perez Gutierrez, 49, said after the violence and repression that led to the Zapatista rebellion, she and other indigenous women responded by organizing and educating themselves about their rights.

"Through this process, we found the need to participate," she said in an interview at the Center for Research and Action for Latin Women. "There were no spaces for women, so we found the need to organize, to participate, and to be valued as women."

Vasquez Boloma, 19, grew up in the Zapatista community of Nueva Jeruselen. She is a trainer with Fray Pedro, educating women and men in workshops as part of a 14-month gender-equality education program.

She said violence against women is widespread. But through training, women are learning to defend themselves.

"Violence comes from everywhere ... there isn't a space where you can say there is no violence," Vasquez Boloma said. "In the house, in the streets, everywhere there is violence. Now that we're receiving workshops, we're going to defend ourselves."

Perez Gutierrez and Vasquez Boloma said men have mixed reactions to women receiving this training. Some are hostile to the idea of women defending themselves.

"They don't like it," Perez Gutierrez said. "They think especially the promoters, they're going to put bad ideas in the heads of women. There's even threats because they don't feel that it's right for the women to defend themselves."

Vasquez Boloma sees the same reaction in her community.

"When they hold a workshop and a woman speaks, the men don't respect her," she said. "Some men think that only men should decide."

Others have come around to the idea.

"Some men have received training and they support us," Vasquez Boloma said. "So things are getting better with men, too."

Perez Gutierrez said she's seen progress in the 21 years she's been fighting for women in Chiapas. The Women's Revolutionary Law helped liberate women, she said.

"I don't have to ask anybody for permission," she said. "Nobody asks me, 'Where are you going?' I make my own decision to leave or to go. I think that's change."

Both women look to future generations to continue the struggle for women's rights in Chiapas.

If she has a daughter someday, Vasquez Boloma envisions for her a dignified life and a tranquil state of mind. Beyond that, she said she has only one wish.

"That she would live free of violence."

In Israel, Ethiopian Immigrants Face High Risk of Partner Violence

Arnon Edelstein

In this viewpoint, Edelstein discusses the roots and realities of intimate partner violence—a kind of honor-based crime—in Ethiopian communities in Israel. Edelstein—a lecturer in criminology who specializes in gender studies and youth at risk—asserts that studying how certain societal conditions and risk factors can breed violence against Ethiopian women is helpful in understanding similar situations for girls and women across the globe.

As you read, consider the following questions:

1. How does racism against Ethiopian immigrants in Israel impact the way they treat one another?
2. What three changes does the author say are risk factors for intimate partner violence against Ethiopian women?
3. What does the plight of Ethiopians in Israel teach us about other immigrant communities around the world?

Addressing the Issue

Dozens of articles and books deal with and try to explain the phenomena of Intimate Partner Violence (IPV) among immigrants, but only a very small part of this literature deals with Intimate Partner Homicide (IPH) among these immigrants (Websdale, 1999; Bent-Goodley, 2007; Carrillo and Zarza 2006; Jin and Keat, 2010;

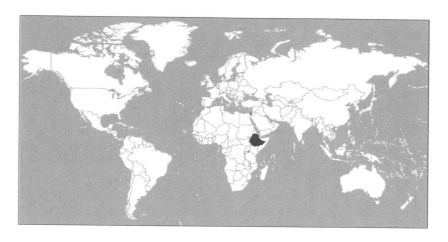

Kasturiangan., Krishnan, and Rieger, S. Kasturirangan et al. 2004; Kim., Lau, and Chang, D.F. Kim et al. 2007; Klevens, 2007; Lee and Handeed, 2009; Morash.,Bui., Zhang and Holtfreter, 2007; Raj and Silverman, 2002; Rodriguez., Valentine and Muhammad, 2009; Vatnar and Bjorkly, 2010; Azezehu-Admasu, 2011; Tavaje, 2011).

Immigrants, mainly from patriarchal cultures, have unique characteristics that differentiate them from other low status populations, and hence, it is fruitful to examine these immigrant traits separately, in order to explain the higher rates of IPV and IPH among them. These crucial differences have to do with: the cultural norms of their original cultures; the acculturation process these immigrants have undergone and the language barriers they must surmount (Carrillo and Zarza 2006; Kim et al., 2007; Klevens, 2007; Rodriguez et al. 2009). Ethiopian immigrant women in Israel, as an example of women who immigrated from a patriarchal society to a modern one, are over-represented as victims of IPH, more than 16 times the rate in the general population (Kacen, 2006; Kacen and Keidar, 2006; Azezehu-Admasu, 2011; Tavaje, 2011). Explanations of this phenomenon coincide with worldwide explanations about IPH against immigrant women from patriarchal societies entering modern ones (Wallach., Weingram and Avitan, 2010; Gal, 2003).

These explanations emphasize the unique role of culture conflict, acculturation and acculturation stress, which place immigrant couples at different levels of acculturation and assimilation into the host society. As a result, immigrant men from patriarchal cultures may be very vulnerable to anger, frustration, depression and despair. These feelings may result in IPH by those with psychological disturbances (Caetano., Ramisetty-Milker., Caetano-Vaeth, and Harris, T.R. 2007;Carrilo and Marza, Carrillo and Zarza Carrillo and Zarza 2006; Kim et al. 2007; Klevens, 2007; Lee and Hadeed, 2009; Morash et al. 2007; Raj and Silverman, 2002; Rodriguez et al. 2009; Azezehu-Admasu, 2011; Tavaje, 2011). In other words, in order to understand IPH against immigrant women, we should adopt social-cultural and psychological points of view.

The Patriarchal Family

Patriarchal family traditions thrive in many underdeveloped countries, independent of whatever political regime is currently in power. For that reason, many of the same cultural characteristics will be found in China, the Vietnams, Ethiopia and other countries (Jin and Keat, 2010; Kim et al. 2007; Klevens, 2007; Morash et al. 2007; Raj and Silverman, 2002; Azezehu-Admasu, 2011; Tavaje, 2011). Rural communities are typically based on expanded families, where age and gender are the crucial variables that grant high social status to the men and the elders. In patriarchal families, there is a clear and rigid division of gender roles and status. The father is the main authority in the family and he is responsible for representing the family in the community. The men are the main breadwinners and, thus, have decision-making privileges regarding financial and other crucial issues in family life. The wife and children are the property of the husband/father and, as such, they must honor and obey him totally. The wives, on the other hand, are deemed responsible for the domestic sphere: cooking, cleaning, laundering, child-rearing and caring for their husbands' needs (Jin and Keat, 2010; Kim et al. 2007; Klevens, 2007; Morash et al. 2007; Raj and Silverman, 2002;Azezehu-Admasu, 2011; Tavaje, 2011). In cases of slight deviance in the behavior of the children or the wife, in patriarchal society, it is considered a legitimate act for the man to punish them forcefully.

Culture in Transition

Immigration to modern societies creates a real threat to patriarchal cultural norms. Modern cultures, on the contrary, can be viewed as a mirror image of patriarchal cultures. Western cultures do not generally appreciate age as an important variable in a person's status; they believe in equality between the genders and in a more flexible division of gender roles. In addition, children in modern societies have many more rights and much greater protection than in the traditional ones (Jin and Keat, 2010; Kim et al. 2007; Klevens, 2007; Morash et al. 2007; Raj and Silverman, 2002).

Most modern countries try to promote the acculturation of newcomers into mainstream culture, but Immigrants from traditional cultures find themselves at the bottom of the socio-economic and ecological ladder of the host society. They lack recourses for upward mobility, such as: second language skills, formal education and professional job skills. They tend to live in poor, socially-disorganized neighborhoods that thwart good community life. Most of these immigrants find themselves in 'ethnic ghettos', in which the male elders try to preserve the culture of origin and their own privileges, as well as the ideology that violence against women is a legitimate and normative way of behavior, to ensure the old social order countries (Jin and Keat, 2010; Kim et al. 2007; Klevens, 2007; Morash et al. 2007; Raj and Silverman, 2002; Azezehu-Admasu, 2011; Tavaje, 2011), (Leherer, 1993).

Racism Against Ethiopians in Israel

Israel is a unique country in that it legislate a special law called "the return law" (1952), which promises that every Jew can immigrate to Israel and have an Israeli citizenship and rights automatically. On the other hand, this formal law does not guarantee that immigrants will get an equalitarian attitude in practical.

Racism is a common phenomenon among immigration countries all over the worled.

Xenophobia is a common trait among citizens who see immigrants as a threat to their well-being, employment, prejudice etc. This phenomenon is more salient against Ethiopian immigrants, due to their different skin color, religious customs, attribution of disease, like H.I.V.

Ethiopian Jews in Israel faced racism in everyday life which shocked them. They were sure that their brothers in Israel will embrace them, but instead, they were referred to the geographical peripheral of Israel, and they suffer from exclusion in every aspect of social life, including political, educational and employment areas.

In addition, after almost 30 years of migration, the Ethiopian Jews are still in the lower class of the Israeli society. There is no doubt that this, in turn, added to the despair of some Ethiopian men.

In fact, it is usually the women and children who are more prepared to explore to their new society and to acculturate, thus improving their status profoundly (Jin and Keat, 2010; Kasturirangan et al. 2004; Klevens, 2007; Morash et al. 2007; Raj and Silverman, 2002). This process results in a reversal of gender roles and statuses which set the women in high risk for violence and even murder by their husbands.

Culture transition among Ethiopians in Israel

In order to better understand the cultural transition among Ethiopians in Israel, we must compare the culture of origin to the Israeli culture and society. The gap between the two is a powerful tool towards understanding the occurrences of Intimate Partner Violence (IPV) and Intimate Partner Homicide (IPH) in this population (Azezehu-Admasu, 2011; Tavaje, 2011).

Social-cultural characteristics of Ethiopian Jews in Ethiopia

In Ethiopia, the Jews lived in rural communities that encompassed several households. The community was based on patriarchal and hierarchic relations. At the head of the socio-religious ladder were the "kesim," who constituted the supreme spiritual leadership (Baharani Barahani 1990; Salomon 1987). At a lower level were the elders of the community ("shimglautz"), whose main function was to maintain the social order by intervention in cases of violation of the common norms. Conflict resolution was handled by arbitration, compromise and by means of orders given to the parties involved in the conflict. In addition, the elders functioned as counselors and mediators between couples, especially after a wife's appeal due to exceptional or prolonged violence by her husband (Kacen, 2006; Sulivan., Senturia., Negash.,, Shiu-Thornton and Giday, B. 2005; Gal, 2003, Kacen and Keidar, 2006; Azezehu-Admasu, 2011; Tavaje, 2011;Bodovsli et al. Bodowski et al. 1994; Finklestin and Solomon Finkrlstein & Solomon, Finklestin and Solomon Finklestin and Solomon 1995; Salomon, 1987).

The communal world-view is that all community affairs belong to the community alone. By the same token, family affairs should be kept among family members, except, perhaps, for involving the elders. As a result, gossiping or telling others about spousal or family problems is considered to be deviant behavior. The same hierarchic structure found in the community was replicated in the family and, therefore, in both settings, the emphasis is on showing respect for the adults, in general, and for the parents, in particular (Weil, 1991; Kacen, 2006; Azezehu-Admasu, 2011; Tavaje, 2011).

The male/husband has a higher status, by definition, because he is a man. Gender roles are very strict, known and clear to everybody. The husband's main functions are supporting his family, disciplining his children and representing his family to outsiders. This supreme status of males also carries the uncompromising authority and dominion of the husband/father over his wife and children, and confers honor upon him, as expressed by the behaviors of his wife and children.

The duty of the wife was to obey her husband's will completely, including having sexual intercourse at his behest. Women functions included childbearing and taking care of the children and the household (Kacen, 2006; Wallach et al. 2010; Gal, 2003).

As part of a patriarchal culture, 'educating' a woman by violent means was considered normative behavior. This behavior seem fair and right in the eyes of the community, including its women (Azezehu-Admasu, 2011; Tavaje, 2011). If a wife argued with her husband, refused to fulfill his wishes or did not prepare his meals- all of these were considered legitimist justifications for wife-beating. In cases of extreme wife-beating or homicidal tendencies, the wife had two options: to escape and return to her original family or to appeal to the elders, so they might treat the violent husband. The elders' decisions were accepted as unquestionable orders. In cases where there was no other solution, the elders could order a divorce (Kacen, 2006).

In summary, spousal violence against a wife in a patriarchal society as in the case of Ethiopian families was considered to be normative behavior, when its purpose was to "educate" the wife regarding her rigid gender role and functions. There were no other reasons for violence against wives, since there was no sexual jealousy or unfaithful behavior in the small communities with their strict social order (Bodovsky., David and Eran, Y. Bodowski et al. 1994; Dolev-Gendelman, 1989; Weil, 1991 1995; Minuchin-Itzikson, 1995;Szold Institution, 1986; Shabtai 1999; Ben Ezer, 1992; Edelstein, 2000; Azezehu-Admasu, 2011; Tavaje, 2011).

[…]

Ethiopians' Culture in Transition

The Ethiopian community experienced three fundamental changes, further increasing the level of stress already inherent in the immigration process. In addition, these changes produced significant risk factors for IPV or IPH against wives.

First, the breakup of extended families into nuclear ones was caused by the dispersal of the original extended families and the separate placement of nuclear families at different locations in Israel, due to the availability of small apartments not suited to a large number of residents. In Ethiopia, the extended family aided and supported the couples. The breakup of this large social unit resulted in the loss of control, regulation and aid mechanisms for men and women alike. The forced transformation of these couples into unsupported nuclear families caused a lot of problems, e.g. women lost their family's support and/or could not run away from spousal violence, to seek refuge in their original families (Kacen, 2006; Sullivan, et al. et al. 2005; Sela-Shayovitz, 2010; Gal, 2003; Kacen and Keidar, 2006; Azezehu-Admasu, 2011; Tavaje, 2011).

The second change relates to the first one and deals with traditional institutions for help. After the immigration to Israel, the status of the "kesim" and the elders decreased significantly. The Israeli Chief Rabbinate did not recognize the authority of the "kes" to serve as rabbi. The authority of the elders also decreased, until their ability to maintain the "old order" in Israeli society became very complicated. This phenomenon occurred in most of the ethnic enclaves where they lived, despite their many attempts to preserve the original culture.

Traditional institutions, like the extended family and the authority of the elders to intervene in marital conflicts, broke down on route and during the absorption process in Israel. As a result, the nuclear unit is more affected by each spouse and more influenced by general Israeli culture (Kacen, 2006; Sullivan et al. 2005; Sela-Shayovitz, 2010; Gal, 2003; Kacen and Keidar, 2006; Azezehu-Admasu, 2011; Tavaje, 2011).

The third and the main change relates to the integration process into Israeli society. Acculturation has implications not only for the individual who undergoes it, but also for his/her relations with others who have not yet acculturated and/or are at a different stage in the process (Scott and Scott, 1989).

Immigrants from Ethiopia lack formal education and professional skills. As a result, the rate of unemployment among them is very high. In addition, Ethiopian men are unemployed for several more reasons: old age, an unwillingness to work at "shameful" jobs, and due to the preference of women in unskilled jobs. As a result the chances for Ethiopian men for successfully acculturate into Israeli society are lower than those of Ethiopian women. In recent years, there has even been a decrease in men's employment, while there is an increase in women's employment (Israeli Association for Ethiopian Jews, 2007). A big effort was made in Israel to empower Ethiopian women by encouraging them to learn Hebrew and to find jobs; yet, no such efforts were made with Ethiopian men (Azezehu-Admasu, 2011; Tavaje, 2011).

The Israeli social-cultural and socio-economic reality has significantly changed the layout of gender roles in relation to the different acculturation paths taken by Ethiopian men and women and/or their being at different stages in the acculturation process. The acculturation process that these women undergo puts them in contact with a more attractive socio-cultural reality than that they had in Ethiopia. They are ones who receive child and other welfare benefits in their bank accounts. They meet well-placed professional Israeli working women, who become their role models. Israeli women "open the Ethiopian women's eyes," as it were, by explaining to them that spousal violence against them is a punishable crime (Shuval, 1979; Kacen, 2006; Sela-Shayovitz, 2010; Kacen and Keidar, 2006; Azezehu-Admasu, 2011; Tavaje, 2011).

In addition, the higher level of Ethiopian women in the acculturation process exposes them to more egalitarian socio-cultural norms in relation to gender roles and interpersonal relationships in Israel. These new revelations seem much preferable to their situation in the traditional patriarchal enclaves. The speedy and successful integration of Ethiopian women into Israeli society creates more cases of men's dependence on their wives, who serve as mediators between their husbands and Israeli society. For Ethiopian couples, this is a profound cultural upheaval, creating bad consequences for men's status and women's safety.

For a husband raised in a "machoistic" culture, in which he was the sole breadwinner and the one who decided the family budget—the transfer of these functions to his wife significantly threatens not only his status as the man of the house, but his own self-perception and public image. Cooley (1902) in his "looking-glass self" theory, said that: "The individual is not what he thinks about himself, he is neither what others think about him, but the individual is what he thinks that the others think he is" (famous paraphrase). In other words, an Ethiopian man fears the loss of status not only within his own nuclear family, but also among other Ethiopian men, who may treat him with disrespect, although they suffer from the same problem. The resulting sense of insecurity has even caused a significant decline in the ability of Ethiopian men to make decisions. Many have become the "passive" partner in the couple, waiting for their wives to come home from work (Bodowski., David and Eran, 1990; Kacen, 2006; Azezehu-Admasu, 2011; Tavaje, 2011).

The familiar way for Ethiopian men to preserve their traditional status and to put women "in their place" is by using those tools they learned in their origin culture, i.e. using violence against them. Although violent wife abuse is generally under-reported to the Police in Israel, an overwhelming percentage those reports are made by abused Ethiopian women (Sela-Shayovitz, 2010).

For Ethiopian men, acculturation means giving up the superior status to women in several areas and a significant loss in personal and social power. As such, the Ethiopian men were not sufficiently motivated to enter Israeli society and their process of acculturation was profoundly damaged. This is an example of "rational choice theory" (Cohen and Felson, 1979), which claims that individuals will choose the possibility that will bring them maximum profit and minimum loss.

Stress Acculturation Among Ethiopian Men in Israel

The three changes mentioned above, are in fact risk factors for IPV and IPH against Ethiopian women, mainly because the severe psychological as well as socio-cultural stress they cast on Ethiopian men. Even those men who begin an acculturation process experience "acculturation stress." It can be said that the objective intercultural differences which are strengthened at the time of absorption, together with the ethnocentric treatment of the immigrants by the absorbers, have led to a traumatic culture shock and acculturation stress as manifested by multiple health problems, in general, and by psychological problems, in particular.

Research done in Israel on Ethiopian and former Soviet immigrants found that immigrants from "Operation Moses" (1984–1985) were more vulnerable to acculturation stress and culture shock than immigrants who came from Ethiopia later on "Operation Solomon" (1991) or than Soviet immigrants (Youngmann., Pugachova, and Zilber, 2009; Ponizovsky., Ginath., Durst., Wondimeneh., Safro., Minuchin- Itzigson and Ritsner, 1998; Youngmann., Minuchin-Itzigson and Barasch, 1999; Finklestin and Solomon). This vulnerability expressed itself by means of psychiatric hospitalizations. There are some explanations for the differences in psychiatric hospitalization between the different immigrants groups. Firstly, immigrants from "Operation Moses" were the spearhead of Ethiopian immigration to Israel and, as a result, suffered the highest levels of culture conflict and culture shock, because of their very different cultural background. Secondly, unlike "Operation Solomon" and former Soviet immigrants, those who came on "Operation Moses" did not have any ready, supportive social network in Israel. They had no advanced delegates in Israel already familiar with the Israeli culture, who could moderate the risk factors of culture shock and acculturation stress (Youngmann et al. 2009).

A direct result of this culture conflict was social disorder. This chaotic situation was manifested at many levels: the community, the extended family, the nuclear family and the individual (Dolev-Gendelman, 1989; Barahani, 1990; Kaplan and Salamon, 1998; Azezehu-Admasu, 2011; Tavaje, 2011; Gresario & Witztum, 1995).

IPV AND IPH Against Ethiopian Immigrant Women "Inconsistency of the Self"

As in cases of other immigrants from patriarchal societies integrating into more modern ones, IPV and IPH are usually explained by the reversal of status and gender roles between husbands and wives in the host society. One of the main psychological reasons for such behaviors is "the inconsistency of the self" (Sullivan et al. 2005) among men who immigrated from patriarchal cultures. This phenomenon can either be a result of interaction with the host society or it may follow the process of change in gender roles and the decline of the man's status (Kacen, 2006; Sela-Shayovitz, 2010; Sullivan et al. 2005; Kacen and Keidar, 2006; Azezehu-Admasu, 2011; Tavaje, 2011).

Psychological theories consider the "consistency of the self" to be a major factor in mental wellbeing. When a person (e.g., an Ethiopian man) feels that everything that was familiar, taken for granted and clear, has changed before his very eyes and he becomes aware of a decline in his personal status, he experiences self-inconsistency. He has difficulty identifying himself in his new situation, where he is passive and dependent, having lost his traditional role and self-perception. These feelings are well documented in the literature and may motivate violent reactions in order to regain the former status and self-image. According to these theories, "inconsistency of the self," in extreme cases, may also raise suicidal thoughts, intentions and actions. This explains the findings that a significant percentage of perpetrators of IPH, mostly Ethiopian husbands, attempt or commit suicide after murdering their wives (Zaharna, 1989).

IPH Triggers Among Ethiopians

When a woman complains about her violent husband to the police and social welfare agencies

This may produce one of two opposite results: either the husband will be deterred by fear of future arrest or he may seek revenge by murdering his wife. As yet, there is no significant data regarding the connection between the lodging of complaints by the wife and IPH, though there is reason to assume it is culturally dependent. Native Ethiopian culture emphasizes the privacy of individuals and family matters. This component becomes even more important after immigration, because of the desire not to stigmatize the community in the eyes of the Israelis. As a result, the rule is not to complain about a violent husband to the Police or welfare workers. This issue should be quietly handled inside the community (Kacen, 2006; Sullivan et al. 2005; Kacen and Keidar, 2006; Azezehu-Admasu, 2011; Tavaje, 2011). Yet, battered Ethiopian women can no longer appeal to the elders or to their extended families and they are encouraged by Israeli women to complain formally against their violent husbands. Many find themselves with no choice, in a situation where they will, for the first time in their life, seek to punish their husbands for the violent abuse against them. Over the years, the number of complaints has grown, indicating that Ethiopian women have learned that violence against them is not merely unacceptable in Israel, but it is a criminal act. In other words, Ethiopian women have acculturated over time.

Being detained, arrested, investigated by the Police, or placed under restraining orders are all considered attacks on the man's honor, humiliations initiated by his wife and further inflicted by his fellowmen, who see him as "no man." Sometimes a restraining order requires the husband to leave his home, making him essentially homeless, because his extended family either does not live nearby or cannot take him into already overcrowded apartments. Still, many battered women are afraid to file complaints against their husbands for cultural reasons: stigmatization by the community, language/communication problems or fear of the husband's reaction.

Ethiopian men, who have been formally accused by their wives, feel very frustrated. They see their wives as deviants, trying to change the laws of nature, not only by ruining their status as men, but by destroying the very core of their honor (Sullivan et al. 2005; Kacen and Keidar, 2006; Sela-Shayovitz, 2010). As such, the filing of a complaint by an Ethiopian wife against her husband is a major trigger for IPH, exacerbated if the man is actually arrested or sentenced to jail. Then, there is a high risk that he will murder her for damaging his honor in such a way. This may be true for men among the general population as well.

The sexual jealousy of Ethiopian men regarding their wives

Sexual jealousy is one of the general triggers in IPH, but among Ethiopian men it is more complicated, due to the socio-cultural changes mentioned above.

More Ethiopian women than men are working outside home. A woman who works meets co-workers (including men) and sometimes stays to work extra hours at her place of employment. In the meantime, her unemployed husband stays at home or with friends, waiting for her. He is not aware of her job, the norms and informal relations that develop in workplaces. He may imagine what his wife is doing for hours without supervision. His low self-esteem, coupled with fears that his wife will leave him, may cause the husband to imagine scripts in which his wife is disloyal to him with another man—an employed man with a better status, maybe an Israeli…somebody better than himself. In some extreme cases, such jealousy may result in IPV and/or IPH. (Azezehu-Admasu, 2011; Tavaje, 2011). Among Ethiopians, this trigger was responsible for 37% of the IPH cases between1990-2010 (Edelstein, 2011).

The willingness of women to leave their intimate relationships

The most important trigger in IPV and/or IPH documented in the literature is the willingness of a woman to leave the relationship she has with her husband, boyfriend or another man. In Israel, this trigger was responsible for 59% of the IPH cases from 1990–2010 (Edelstein, 2011). Ethiopian wives, who are more acculturated than their husbands, no longer want to stay with a violent husband. They have not only learned that this behavior is criminal, but they now understand that they have another option, which they did not have before.

As the DSM-IV shows, some individuals suffer from low self-esteem, abandonment anxiety and dependence in others. Every real or imagine sign that they might left alone, provoke a psychological reaction, in order to survive this threat. For Ethiopian men who became dependent and has abandonment anxiety, their wives' leaving symbolizes disaster.

Not only will the woman damage her husband's "personal honor" making him an undesirable man, but she will damage his "social honor" among his fellowmen. In addition, unemployed husbands, who do not know Hebrew, feel that they are being abandoned, left alone in an incomprehensible, alien world (Ben Ezer, 1989; Kacen, 2006). Thus, some Ethiopian murderers act out of rage against the woman who wants to harm them so much. On another psychological level, men with dependent personalities and/or abandonment anxiety will view the woman's will as a major threat to their existence. By murdering their wives, these husbands are trying to prevent them from leaving; some of these murderers will commit suicide. Among Ethiopians, this trigger was responsible for 50% of IPH cases from 1990–2010. In 50% of these IPH cases, the murderer also attempted or committed suicide (Edelstein, 2011). As the literature shows, fear of abandonment is the most risky trigger for IPH; most husbands who murdered their wives, did so during in the first year after the breakup of their marriage (Kacen, 2006; Sela-Shayovitz, 2010; Kacen and Keidar, 2006; Morash et al. 2007). In my opinion, being reported for wife-abuse to the authorities or spousal infidelity (real or imagined) produce temporary situations; however, the breakup of a marriage or relationship is final, chaotic and results in hopelessness. Its finality is also its lethality.

[...]

Summary and Conclusions

Immigration from a patriarchal culture into a more egalitarian one produces many risk factors for IPH. One of these significant risk factors is derived from the acculturation process, which provides two relevant explanations for the occurrence of IPH among Ethiopian immigrants to Israel. First of all, acculturation stress may be responsible for some of the psycho-social disorders witnessed in new Ethiopian immigrants. Secondly, dislocation is caused between the Ethiopian men and women in the level they have achieved in the acculturation process; as long as the women more quickly attain higher levels than the men in this process, we can expect to see more cases of IPV and IPH. The acculturation process clashes, in many ways, with the norms, perceptions and behaviors which were taken for granted in the original culture. The resulting reversal of gender roles and status between men and women causes one of the main risk factors among these immigrants.

In addition to the general risk factors known in the general population, there are unique risk factors among immigrants from patriarchal societies. The acculturation process escalates the violence by certain men, when they attempt to preserve their former status. Nonetheless, Ethiopian women in modern Israeli society have new recourses and new reactions to counter violent abuse against them that they never had before in Ethiopia. They can now go to the Israeli authorities to report their husbands' deeds and to seek protection. Alternatively, the fact that more immigrant women have learned the Hebrew language and, thus, hold jobs encourages them to leave their violent relationships or to keep their husbands at a distance by getting restraining orders, and so on.

There are additional triggers, stressors, that add to the risk factors mentioned above, that apply to these new immigrants, whose suffering paves the men's way to committing the murders of their intimate partners, as we have seen in the case study.

One of our conclusions is that we cannot separate the socio-cultural and psychological factors. We have studied the direct impacts of acculturation, acculturation stress, inconsistency of the self, despair and other psychological disorders, all of which plague these immigrants, and concluded that only an integrative model may provide a whole picture of IPH.

Ethiopians who immigrated to Israel are not different from other immigrants from patriarchal cultures. For this reason, they provide an empirical example of the various processes experienced these immigrants. Although the Ethiopian culture is unique and the Ethiopians have special traits as Jews in Israel, they still exhibit the same problems documented in the literature regarding other immigrants to the U.S.

[...]

References

Anderman LF: Ethiopian Jews meet Israeli family physicians: A study of Cultural somatization. Transcult Psychiatry 1996, 13(3):333-345.

Arieli A: Persecutory experience and posttraumatic stress disorder among Ethiopian immigrants. In Grief and Bereavement in Contemporary Society. Edited by: Ghigier E. London: Freund Publications; 1988:70-76.

Arieli A, Gilat I, Eyzek Z: Suicide of Ethiopian Jews. Medicine 1994, 127: 3-4.

Azezehu-Admasu D: Attitudes and point of views of violent and non-violent Ethiopian immigrant men concerning domestic violence and murder among the Ethiopian community in Israel. Master thesis, Bar Ilan University: department of criminology; 2011.

Barahani Z: Family and community life of the Jews in Ethiopia and during the transition to Israel. In Problems in the Care of Families from Different Cultural Backgrounds. Edited by: Bodowski D, Eran DY. Jerusalem: IAEJ (Hebrew); 1990:3-5-16.

Ben- Ezer G: Ethiopian immigrants and their absorption in Israel. Monthly Review. Monthly Rev 1989, 36(3):37-41. Hebrew

Ben- Ezer G: Like Light in the Pitcher. Jerusalem: R. Mass (Hebrew); 1992.

Ben- Ezer G: The Ethiopian Jewish Exodus. London: Routledge Pub. Co.; 2002.

Ben-David E: Europe's shifting immigration dynamic. Middle East Q 2009, 16(2):15-24.

Bent-Goodley TB: Health disparities and violence against women: Why and how cultural and societal influences matter. Trauma Violence Abuse 2007, 8(2):90-104. 10.1177/1524838007301160

Berry JW, Kim U, Minde Y, Mok D: Comparative studies of acculturation stress. Int Migrat Rev 1987, 21: 491-511. 10.2307/2546607

Bodowski D, David Y, Eran Y: Problems in the Care of Families from a Different Cultural Background. IAEJ (Hebrew): Jerusalem; 1990.

Bodowski D, David Y, Eran Y: Ethiopian Jewry in Inter-Cultural Transition: The Family and the Life Cycle. IAEJ (Hebrew): Jerusalem; 1994.

Caetano R, Ramisetty-Milker S, Caetano-Vaeth P, Harris TR: Acculturation stress, drinking and intimate partner violence among Hispanic couples in the U.S. J Interpers Violence 2007, 22(11):1431-1447. 10.1177/0886260507305568

Carrillo R, Zarza MJ: An intervention model for Latino perpetrators of intimate partner violence. Habana: VII Congreso International de Desastres; 2006.

Cohen LE, Felson M: Social change and crime rate trends: A routine activities approach. Am Sociol Rev 1979, 44: 588-608. 10.2307/2094589

Cooley CH: Human Nature and the Social Order. New York: Scribner; 1902.

Dawson JL: Theory and method in biosocial psychology. Annals 1977, 25: 46-65.

Dolev-Gendelman T: Ethiopian Jewry in Israel: Family Pictures. Jerusalem: Hebrew University, Institute for Study of Fostering in Education (Hebrew); 1989.

Edelstein A Ph. D. Thesis. In Patterns of Delinquency and Social Deviance among Ethiopian Jewish Youth in Israel. Jerusalem: Hebrew University, Institute of Criminology (Hebrew); 2000.

Edelstein A: Multiple Victim Murder. Beersheba: Ben-Gurion University of the Negev Press (Hebrew); 2009.

Edelstein A: Intimate Partner Homicide in Israel. Beersheba: Ben-Gurion University of the Negev Press (Hebrew); 2011. forthcoming

Engel GL: The need for a new medical model: a challenge for biomedicine. Science 1977, 196: 129-36. 10.1126/science.847460

Engel GL: The clinical application of the biopsychosocial model. Am J Psychiatry 1980, 137: 535-544.

Faberga H: The role of culture in a theory of psychiatric illness. Soc Sci Med 1992, 35(1):91-103. 10.1016/0277-9536(92)90122-7

Finklestin M, Solomon Z: Cumulative Trauma, PTSD and Dissociation among Ethiopian Refugees in Israel. London: Routledge; 1995.

Gal N: Violence against Women: Norm or Deviance?. Tel-Aviv: United Kibbutz Press (Hebrew); 2003.

Giel R: Some observations on Ethiopian psychiatry. Isr J Psychiatry Relat Sci 1986, 23(1):39-48.

Goldstein MS, Jaffe DT, Sutherland C, Wilson J: Holistic Physicians: implication for the study of the medical profession. J Health Soc Behav 1987, 28: 103-119. 10.2307/2137125

Gresario N: Doctor, I have worms in my head: Mental problems of Ethiopians in Israel. Psychiatr Med 2010, 131: 28-35.

Gresario N, Witztum E: The zar phenomenon among Ethiopian immigrants in Israel. Conversations 1995, 9(3):209-220. Hebrew

Halper J: The absorption of Ethiopian immigrants: A return to the fifties. Isr Soc Sci Res J 1985, 3(1–2):112-139.

Herzog A: Zoo of absorption activists. Ve`adim [Committees]. 1992, 38-39. Hebrew

Google Scholar

Herzog A: Bureaucracy and the Ethiopian Immigrants. Tel Aviv: Cherikover Publishers (Hebrew); 1998.

Hodes RM: Cross-cultural medicine and misunderstanding: The case of the Ethiopians. West J Med 1997, 166: 29-36.

Israel Association for Ethiopian Jews: Ethiopian Immigrants in Israel in the Labor Market. IAEJ (Hebrew): Jerusalem; 2007.

Jin X, Keat JE: The effects of change in spousal power on intimate partner violence among Chinese immigrants. J Interpers Violence 2010, 25(4):610-625. 10.1177/0886260509334283

Kacen L: Spousal abuse among immigrants from Ethiopia in Israel. J Marriage Fam 2006, 68: 1276-1290. 10.1111/j.1741-3737.2006.00328.x

Kacen L, Keidar L: Violence between Couples among Ethiopian Families in Israel. Welfare Ministry (Hebrew): Jerusalem Israel; 2006.

Kaplan S, Salamon H: Ethiopian immigrants in Israel: Experience and prospects. Institute for Jewish Policy Research, 1. London: IJPR; 1998.

Kasturirangan A, Krishnan S, Rieger S: The impact of culture and minority status on women's experience of domestic violence. Trauma Violence Abuse 2004, 4(4):318-332.

Kim IJ, Lau AS, Chang DF: Handbook of Asian American Psychology, Ch. 21. Thousand Oaks: Sage Publications; 2007.

Klevens J: An overview of intimate partner violence among Latinos. Violence Against Women 2007, 13(2):111-122. 10.1177/1077801206296979

Lee YS, Hadeed L: Intimate partner violence among Asian immigrant Communities. Trauma Violence Abuse 2009, 10(2):143-170. 10.1177/1524838009334130

Leherer Z: The Psychology of Immigration. Tel-Aviv: I.D.F. Press (Hebrew); 1993.

Minuchin-Itzikson S: Anthropological description of the meeting between the cultures of the Ethiopian Jews (Falashas) and Israeli culture. Leaves 1995, 5: 15-21. Hebrew

Morash M, Bui H, Zhang Y, Holtfreter K: Risk factors for abusive relationships: A study of Vietnamese American immigrant women. Violence Against Women 2007, 13(7):653-675. 10.1177/1077801207302044

Ponizovsky A, Ginath Y, Durst R, Wondimeneh B, Safro S, Minuchin-Itzigson , Ritsner M: Psychological distress among Ethiopian and Russian Jewish immigrants to Israel: A cross-cultural study. Int J Soc Psychiatry 1998, 44(1):35-45. 10.1177/002076409804400104

View ArticleGoogle Scholar

Posner Y: The mediation plan: Summary report. Jerusalem: J.D.C. (Hebrew); 1996.

Raj A, Silverman J: Violence against immigrant women. Violence Against Women 2002, 8(3):367-398. 10.1177/10778010222183107

Rodriguez M, Valentine JM, Muhammad M: Intimate partner violence and barriers to mental health care for ethnically diverse populations of women. Trauma Violence Abuse 2009, 10(4):358-374. 10.1177/1524838009339756

Rosen H: Disease, Healing and Healers: The Traditional Ethiopian Perspective and its Relevance for Health in Israel Today. Lod: Habermann Institute; 1985.

Salamon H: Travels as a means of communication among the Beta Israel [Jews] in Ethiopia. Steps 1987, 33: 109-123. Hebrew

Scott WA, Scott R: Adaption of immigrants: individual differences and determinants. Oxford: Pergamum Press; 1989.

Scott MB, Lyman S: Accounts. In Life as Theater: a Dramaturgical Sourcebook. Edited by: Brisset D, Edgley C. Chicago: Aldine Pub. Co.; 1990:219-238.

Sela-Shayovitz R: The role of ethnicity and context: Intimate femicide rates among social groups in Israeli society. Violence Against Women 2010, 16(2):1424-1436.

Shabtai M: Indeed My Brother: The Voyage of Identity of Soldiers of Ethiopian Origin. Tel-Aviv: Cherikover Publishers (Hebrew); 1999.

Shuval JT: Migration and stress. In Handbook of Stress: Theoretical and Clinical Aspects. Edited by: Goldberger L, Breznitz S. London: Free Press; 1979.

Sullivan M, Senturia K, Negash T, Shiu-Thornton S, Giday B: For us it is like living in the dark. J Interpers Violence 2005, 20(8):922-940. 10.1177/0886260505277678

Szold Institute: Ethiopian Jewry and Their Absorption in Israel. Jerusalem: Szold Institute (Hebrew); 1986.

Tafari S, Aboud FE, Larson CP: Determinants of mental illness in a rural Ethiopian adult population. Soc Sci Med 1991, 32: 197-201. 10.1016/0277-9536(91)90060-P

Tavaje W: Violence against women in the Ethiopian community in Israel: Perspectives of partner perpetrated domestic violence. Master thesis, Bar Ilan university: department of criminology; 2011.

Vatnar SK, Bjorkly S: An interactional perspective on the relationship of immigration to intimate partner violence in a representative sample of help- seeking women. J Interpers Violence 2010, 25(10):1815-1835. 10.1177/0886260509354511

Wallach HS, Weingram Z, Avitan O: Attitudes toward domestic violence: A cultural perspective. J Interpers Violence 2010, 25(7):1284-1297. 10.1177/0886260509340540

View ArticleGoogle Scholar

Websdale N: Understanding Domestic Homicide. Boston: Northeastern University Press; 1999.

Weil S: One-Parent Families among Ethiopian Immigrants in Israel. Jerusalem: Hebrew University, Institute for the Study of Fostering in Education (Hebrew); 1991.

Weil S: Ethiopian Jews in the limelight. Isr Soc Sci Res 1995, 10(2):3-7.

Williams CL, Berry JW: Primary prevention of acculturation stress among refugees. Am Psychol 1991, 46(6):632-641.

Yassour Y: The Decision to Kill. Tel-Aviv: Ramot Press (Hebrew); 1995.

Young A: Internalizing and externalizing medical belief systems: An Ethiopian example. Soc Sci Med 1976, 10: 147-156. 10.1016/0037-7856(76)90041-X

Youngmann R, Minuchin-Itzikson S, Barasch M: Manifestations of emotional distress among Ethiopian immigrants in Israel: Patient and clinical perspectives. Transcult Psychiatry 1999, 36(1):45-63. 10.1177/136346159903600103

Youngmann R, Pugachova I, Zilber N: Patterns of psychiatric hospitalization among Ethiopian and Former Soviet Union immigrants and persons born in Israel. 2009. See http://psychservices.psychiatryonline.org/archive/60(12): 1656–1663 [last viewed March 2011]

Zaharna RS: Self-shock: The double-binding challenge of Identity. Int J Intercult Relat 1989, 13: 501-525. 10.1016/0147-1767(89)90026-6

In the United Kingdom, Cultural and Gender Issues Behind Honor Killing Must Not Be Ignored

Rupa Reddy

In the following viewpoint, Rupa Reddy says that cases of honor violence must be assessed on an individual basis, with particular attention to cultural implications. Reddy argues that a balanced approach is beneficial to protecting victims and preventing further violence. Reddy, who studies and writes about gender violence issues in immigrant communities, says that it is important to prevent stereotyping or stigmatizing by implying that gender-based violence occurs only among immigrant communities..

As you read, consider the following questions:

1. Besides honor killing, which other issue associated with honor violence is the United Kingdom acting upon?
2. What is multiculturalism?
3. How does provocation impact honor killing cases?

Introduction

In the UK today there is an increasing focus on honour-related violence within ethnic minority communities, whereby the professed or alleged motivation for the violence revolves around a perceived violation of male or family "honour."[1] A number

"Gender, Culture and the Law: Approaches to 'Honour Crimes' in the UK", by Rupa Reddy, Springer, October 24, 2008. Reprinted by permission.

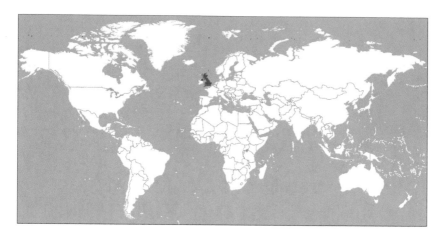

of recent high-profile cases of so-called "honour killings" have received unprecedented media attention and have caused much debate on the subject of how to prevent and punish such crimes. Additionally, the issue of forced marriages has been highlighted by attempts to introduce criminal or civil sanctions specifically aimed at combating them.[2]

    This article will examine the extent to which "honour" should be interpreted either in the context of cultural tradition, or as an aspect of broader, cross-cultural, gender-based violence. It argues that a nuanced approach to the relative roles of culture and gender in the perpetration of "honour crimes" is necessary, in order to ensure effective protection from and prevention of such violence. Analysis of recent UK cases involving "honour killings" and forced marriages illustrates how the legal system can be complicit in upholding or even promoting views of "honour" as primarily or purely cultural, rather than as motivated by patriarchal or other values. However, the possibility that the courts are beginning to incorporate more of a gender-based approach may also be emerging.

"Honour Crimes": Gender Violence?

Whilst it is beyond the scope of this article to fully dissect the various conceptualisations of "honour" and honour-related violence,[3] for the present purposes it is adequate to state that the term "honour killing," though much debated, envisages a scenario where usually (but not always) a woman is killed to either prevent or repair perceived violations of male or familial "honour." The latter include not only perceived sexual impropriety, but also any behaviour not approved of by family members and seen as challenging to patriarchal authority (Touma-Sliman 2005, p. 186; Araji 2000, p. 3). A number of scholars and activists also theorise forced marriage as both a type of "honour crime" in itself, and the precursor to or result of other types of honour-related violence (Welchman and Hossain 2005, p. 4). Forced marriage may lead to ongoing marital rape, as the lack of consent to the marriage may be paralleled by ongoing lack of consent to sexual relations (Siddiqui 2003, pp. 88–89). Once married, attempts to escape from a forced marriage are often the catalyst for further violence including "honour killing" (Siddiqui 2000, p. 50). Forced marriage may also be used to prevent women from exercising a range of autonomous behaviour or actions such as attempting to choose their own partner. Thus women may also be "forced out" of a marriage which they have freely chosen to enter (Chakravarti 2005, p. 308).

"Honour" is constructed through dualistic notions of male "honour" and female "shame," whereby masculinity is largely constructed in terms of female chastity. Conceptions of "honour" are tied to male self-worth and social worth, but most closely in relation to the reputation and social conduct of female family members (Spierenburg 1998, p. 2; Araji 2000, p. 2). Men retain masculine self-worth not only through the regulation and disciplining of the behaviour of their female relatives, but also by protecting them from potential dishonouring by other males (Lindisfarne 1994, p. 85; Goksel 2006, p. 56). Historically, including in the European context, this has been linked to ideas of women as the property of their male relatives, which again results in attempts to control female behaviour, particularly female sexual autonomy (Bashar 1983, pp. 30–32; Harris 1989, p. 299; Clark 1989, p. 231; Clark 1983, p. 14). "Shame" is redressed through punishment of the deviant female (Araji 2000, p. 4), and the alleged "shame" caused by such actions can be "washed away" through the eradication of the source of the "shame"—the woman. In fact if men do not attempt to repair or renew the male family "honour" in this way they are seen as emasculated (Gilmore 1987, p. 10; Abu-Odeh 1996, p. 152). Women are viewed as chattels, conduits through which male property is to be passed, and to be disposed of or controlled for this purpose. Women and children are thus dehumanised, making it easier to justify violent behaviour towards them if they attempt to resist or undermine this patriarchal structure through their actions (Hassan 1999, p. 590).

"Honour" codes depend largely upon control and objectification of women, and the maintenance of strict codes of gendered behaviour to police concepts of "shame" and property associated with female sexuality. Thus "honour" adheres differentially, and unequally to men and women. Women are responsible not only for their own "honour," but for that of their male family members, and women who transgress "honour" codes are treated far more harshly than their male counterparts (Baker et al. 1999, p. 168). Sen (2005, p. 48) argues that "codes of honour serve to construct not only what it means to be a woman but also what it means to be a man, and hence are central to social meanings of gender". Likewise, other authors note that the upholding of "honour" is inextricably aligned with concepts of masculinity (Spierenburg 1998). Women are undoubtedly the primary victims of "crimes of honour" at the hands of largely male perpetrators (Welchman and Hossain 2005, p. 6; Sen 2005, p. 48). Additionally, concepts of "honour" and "shame" largely revolve around female sexuality, and violence against women in general has been closely linked to the regulation of female sexuality (Coomaraswamy 2005a, p. xi). For these reasons, it would seem appropriate to classify such crimes as a form of gender-based violence against women.

A major difficulty with the framing of honour-related violence as a gendered abuse is the issue of male victims of such violence. According to the non-governmental organisation Southall Black

Sisters, in the UK context there have been attempts by politicians and governmental officials to argue that such violence is gender-neutral, since men have been the victims of "honour killings" and forced marriages (Siddiqui 2003, p. 71). This is indeed the case, and at least one major legal case on forced marriage in the Scottish family courts has involved a male petitioner.[4] Nevertheless, Siddiqui argues that even where men suffer forced marriage it is still easier for them to escape from the situation. Women, by contrast, face far greater pressure to reconcile themselves to abusive situations and to suffer ongoing abuse (Siddiqui 2003, p. 71; Araji 2000, p. 5; Baker et al. 1999, p. 168). Men are more easily able to escape the negative sanctions triggered by a breach of "honour," and even if they are subject to violence, their female counterparts still do not escape punishment themselves (Baker et al. 1999, p. 168). Even cases where men are the victims of an "honour killing" usually occur because the victim is alleged to have ruined a woman's reputation by reneging on a promise of marriage, or through an actual or suspected relationship with her (Siddiqui 2005, p. 264). In this way, without attempting to simply dismiss or deny the victimisation of males in certain cases, it is still possible to argue that their victimisation revolves around attempts to control women, and that it is a form of gender-based violence.[5]

However, beyond this analysis there are also broader issues of gender and sexuality that require examination. For example, gay women may suffer honour-related violence if their sexual orientation becomes known and is deemed to bring shame or dishonour to their family or community.[6] Under the analysis set out above, such honour-related violence results from patriarchal attempts to control women's behaviour, particularly sexual behaviour. However, this alone would not explain why gay men may also be targets of honour-related violence, for reasons of their sexual orientation alone, and without any attachment to a female victim to provide a motivator for violence.[7] Therefore arguably honour codes, and any resultant violence, are concerned not only with the upholding of patriarchal heterosexual norms in relation to women, but also of broader norms of heteronormativity which affect both men and women more generally.[8] In conjunction with this, male competition over masculinity and attempts to dominate in the masculine hierarchy may also affect some men, as well as women, in relation to honour codes (Lindisfarne 1994, p. 85). Whilst it is beyond the scope of this article to fully address the wider issues of masculinity and sexuality potentially underlying honour-related violence, it is to be hoped that this brief discussion of their relevance highlights the need for more detailed debate in the near future.

"Honour Crimes" Within a Multicultural Context

In contrast with this gender-based approach to the problem of "honour crimes," is that which argues that such crimes are more specifically located within certain cultures. This is very relevant within the multicultural context of the UK, where reporting of such crimes has to date only taken place in relation to ethnic minority communities. The definition of multiculturalism varies according to context and jurisdiction, but in the UK, multiculturalism was introduced with the aim of combating racism at the same time as promoting an integrated, tolerant and egalitarian society, where the diversity of cultures and races are valued equally (Patel 2000, p. 6). However, problems may arise where the minority cultures in question disagree with egalitarian principles espoused by the majority community, including in relation to the treatment of women (Cohen et al. 1999, p. 4). Feminist theorists argue that multiculturalism pays more attention to the differences between groups than within them, and that consequently, power imbalances within groups are left unquestioned (Okin 1999, p. 12; Patel 2000, p. 7; Siddiqui 2005, pp. 271, 278). Indeed, attempts to create equality and tolerance between groups may unwittingly serve to actively reinforce power hierarchies within groups, leaving already disempowered members further vulnerable to injustice in a "paradox of multicultural vulnerability" (Shachar 2001, pp. 2–3).

Multiculturalist discourses often assume minority communities to be homogenous, with static or fixed cultures (Bhavnani 1993, p. 38; Patel 2000, pp. 6–7; Volpp 2001, p. 1191). It has been argued that the focus on the differences between groups encourages the idea that cultures are monolithic or reified, rather than evolving and open to debate from within (Okin 1999, p. 12). But this begs the question, raised by feminists and others, of what is meant by the term "culture" and who decides its meaning (Okin 1999, p. 12; Pollit 1999, p. 28). The strengthening of existing dominant sub-groups which can result from multicultural policy means that dissenting voices are less able to contribute to the construction or interpretation of what is meant by "culture" (Tamir 1999, p. 47). This is a particularly important debate in the context of honour-related violence, because "honour crimes" have been described as "cultural traditions" or practices which are somehow innate to certain communities. For example, in its attempts to avoid being seen as racist or Islamophobic after the terrorist attacks of 11 September 2001, the Council of Europe stated that "honour crimes" emanate from cultural rather than religious roots.[9]

Such viewpoints add to the perception of culture as fixed and immutable, rather than selected according to context by powerful members of a group in order to preserve existing power structures such as gender hierarchies (Bauer and Helie 2006, pp. 71–72). This overlooks the possibility of resistance or contestation within groups as to the nature of "culture" (Volpp 2001, pp. 1192–1193). The contingent nature of culture is specifically shown in the multicultural context by the fact that those within minority cultures are able, to varying degrees, to navigate the majority culture as well as their own. As Ballard (1994, p. 31) argues in relation to the ability of second generation South Asian migrants in the UK to negotiate different cultural arenas, "Cultures, like languages, are codes, which actors use to express themselves in a given context; and as the context changes, so those with the requisite competence simply switch code".

This context-based analysis is relevant because it indicates that cultures are neither closed nor necessarily always imposed.

Thus identity, including cultural identity, can be "chosen, and actively used, albeit within particular social contexts and restraints" (Bulmer and Solomos 1998, p. 826). This is particularly revealing in the case of alleged "cultural traditions," because it offers the prospect of individual agency within certain circumstances. It may help to explain why the majority of those within communities affected by such traditions still do not carry them out, despite the allegedly inflexible nature of the practices in question. Linked to this, it may be that an explanation for those incidents of violent behaviour that do occur, is that the victim is perceived to have navigated "too far" out of accepted cultural restraints, or without "code-switching competence" in certain contexts. Furthermore, if culture is thus not necessarily as oppressive or all-encompassing as is often argued, then other, more cross-cultural dynamics such as patriarchal ones may also be at work in dictating behaviours, including violent ones.

The focus on immigrant cultures as determined by violence against women supposes that the culture of the dominant society is inherently less patriarchal and violent towards women, and fails to sufficiently interrogate patriarchal practices that exist in majority or Western cultures. So in the dominant society, gender violence is assumed to be the work of individual deviants rather than emanating from cultural beliefs or traditions, with the effect that only immigrant women suffer "death by culture" (Volpp 2001, pp. 1187, 1190). The view that culture belongs only to non-Western societies is problematic, since it results in a failure to interrogate the (erroneous) idea that majority groups are somehow neutral or lacking in culture. The refusal by some Western feminists to accept the contingent nature of cultural norms also leads to an at least implicit assertion of superiority over women of other cultures, and diverts attention from the subordination of women within their own culture (Volpp 2001, p. 1214; Prins and Saharso 2006, p. 6). Culturally-focused responses to issues such as honour-related violence may ultimately prove counterproductive, causing communities to turn further inwards and reinforce the practices in question, in part as a response to fear for their survival, cultural or otherwise, as a community (An-Na'im 2000). They could also have the effect of providing "windows of opportunities for racist and xenophobic actors and organisations" to manipulate the discourse around such crimes in order to further anti-immigration agendas (Hellgren and Hobson 2006, pp. 1–2).[10] Thus, there is a need for caution in associating "honour crimes" with particular minority communities, because of the risk that this could lead to stereotyping and stigmatisation of communities as backward or "other," especially in the post-September 11 context of Islamophobia (Welchman and Hossain 2005, pp. 13–14; Sen 2005, p. 44).

However, to completely ignore cultural issues in relation to violence against women may also lead to a lack of contextualisation, and the potential for compounding the discrimination faced by minority women. Appropriate acknowledgment of cultural context can potentially benefit female victims of violence if it adds to an understanding of the specific nature of the difficulties they face. The problem does not lie with the acknowledgment of cultural contexts and factors per se, but rather with the importance given to them, and the uses to which they are put, in the assessment of theoretical and practical responses to violence against women. One such approach would balance the rights of women and equality within groups, against the aims of diversity and equity between groups. However, others argue that where violence is involved, cultural factors should not be taken into account if to do so would undermine women's fundamental rights. UK activists such as Southall Black Sisters have described this approach as a "mature multiculturalism" whereby acts of violence against women are "understood as abuses and violations of women's fundamental human rights, irrespective of the cultural or religious contexts in which they occur" (Women Against Fundamentalism and Southall Black Sisters 2007, p. 17). They argue that this would help to address problems relating to gender power imbalances, including violence against women, which are compounded by the focus of multiculturalism on relations between, rather than within, groups (Siddiqui 2005, p. 271). One advantage of the "mature multiculturalism" approach is that it nonetheless recognises the many benefits of multicultural policy, and argues for its redefinition rather than outright rejection (Patel 2008, pp. 11–12). Specifically, this redefinition could take the form of deconstructing preconceived notions of culture as bounded and reified (rather than rejecting notions of culture altogether), whilst still retaining the more positive aspects of multiculturalism.[11]

A question raised by the phrase "irrespective of (the) cultural or religious context(s)", is whether it could be interpreted by critics of the "mature multiculturalism" approach as a requirement to preclude the acknowledgment of any cultural issues, even where it may be necessary to do so in order to ensure the best possible outcome for a woman suffering from violence. For example, the use of cultural evidence in cases of women who have killed abusive partners could be crucial in informing the court as to the ways in which issues such as gender and culture can intersect to compound and alter the difficulties women face in attempting to escape violence. However, this presents a further question, which is that if cultural evidence is used to the benefit of women then arguably it should also be available to male defendants, which could result in further injustice to female victims. On what basis, then, is the decision as to when to allow such evidence made? One possibility is that if violence against women such as honour-related violence is viewed as gender-based to a greater extent than it is viewed as cultural, then the gender discrimination intrinsic to such violence becomes a key factor in deciding whether to allow such evidence.

Related to this is whether the "mature multiculturalism" approach inadvertently perpetuates earlier suggestions by feminist theorists of an intractable conflict between gender and reified concepts of culture (Okin 1999, p. 22). The question then arises as to whether "there is a limit to the practices or behaviours that can be condoned in any given society, and if so, what justifies this limit?" (Phillips 2007, p. 32). However, as Phillips argues, it is uncontroversial to suggest that the principles limiting multicultural accommodation should include the protection of minors from harm, the prevention of mental and physical violence, and gender equality (2007, p. 34). Given the current media and governmental focus on these abuses in the UK, it is unlikely that even the most conservative of community leaders or members would now openly or directly advocate "honour killings" or forced marriages, or claim that they were cultural traditions which they have a 'right' to continue with. Thus, it is not a question of crudely balancing the rights of women to be free from violence against cultural rights.[12] Rather, the problem lies with the more subtle way in which multicultural policy facilitates communities in claiming that the problem is not as acute as is being claimed, and that if there is a problem, it is being adequately managed within the community. Furthermore, the government and its agencies, such as the police, may hesitate to intervene for fear of accusations of racism (Siddiqui 2000, p. 51; Patel 2000, pp. 6–7; Siddiqui 2005, p. 270). The result is that responsibility for tackling abuses such as "honour killings" is evaded, and the protection of women is, although more subtly, nonetheless superseded by multicultural concerns (Patel 2008, p. 18).

A final question is how the "mature multiculturalism" approach is applicable in practice in protecting women in ethnic minority communities from gender violence. Conceptually the "mature multiculturalism" approach appears similar to cross-cultural or universalistic approaches to women's human rights.[13] However, there may be differences in the way these approaches can be implemented within the law. The latter approach would seek to rely on the principles in the Human Rights Act 1998 (HRA)[14] to protect victims of gender violence. However, in the UK context of gender violence, the protection offered by the HRA relies on the extent to which the principles contained therein create not only "vertical" obligations between the individual and the state (in the form of public authorities, such as police and prosecution authorities), but also "horizontal" obligations between individuals and non-state actors who are outside state machinery.[15] Although there is growing support amongst activists and scholars for the existence of positive or "horizontal" obligations in relation to domestic violence (using the argument that the state machinery has failed in its obligations to adequately respond to and prevent domestic violence between private individuals), the jurisprudence on this issue is still developing.[16] In relation to honour-related violence, it also requires a conceptualisation of such violence as part of a broader spectrum of gender violence, rather than as culturally differentiated from it, as is largely the case at present in the UK. Thus, whilst the discourse of women's human rights will undoubtedly be of great importance in the future, it is currently of somewhat limited assistance in protecting potential victims of "honour crimes" in the UK. The "mature multiculturalism" approach, whilst not formally embodied in the law in the same way as the provisions of the HRA, nonetheless still represents a gender-focused approach to the protection of women from violence, including honour-related violence, which may be incorporated into judicial understandings and interpretations. The next section will demonstrate how this approach is being used by the courts in cases of forced marriages, in substance if not explicitly. However, in cases of "honour killings" in which the defence of provocation has been raised, a more culturally-focused approach prevails at the expense of sensitivity to broader issues of gender violence.

"Honour Crimes" in the UK Courts

This final section will examine the impact of some of these issues on UK case law pertaining to honour-related violence. In cases of "honour killing," cultural evidence may be relevant where the defendant attempts to plead not guilty to murder, but instead guilty to manslaughter by reason of provocation. In order to establish the defence of provocation both a subjective and an objective test must be satisfied. The subjective element determines whether the evidence shows that there was in fact a sudden and temporary loss of self-control on the part of the defendant. The objective element of the test revolves around whether the alleged provocation was such that a reasonable man would have acted in the same way as the defendant. A succession of cases have struggled with this latter aspect of provocation, and in particular, with the question of what particular characteristics of the defendant can be imputed to the reasonable man in deciding whether he would have lost self-control and killed the victim in the same circumstances.[17] Overturning the earlier ruling in *Bedder*,[18] the House of Lords in *Camplin*[19] decided that since "the gravity of verbal provocation may well depend on the particular characteristics and circumstances" of the defendant, some characteristics could be taken into account. However, only characteristics which bear on the *gravity* of the provocation should be taken into account, whereas characteristics bearing on the accused's *level of self-control* should not. So if the provocation was based on taunts as to the defendant's impotence, then this characteristic of the defendant may be taken into account in assessing whether the gravity of the provocation was severe enough to provoke a reasonable man in his position; however, it may not be taken into account in determining the level of self-control a reasonable man, and therefore the defendant, should possess. The court deemed that the only exceptions to this distinction were the characteristics of age and sex, which could be relevant to both the gravity of the provocation and the expected standard of self-control.

In relation to "honour killings," the question is whether cultural background or belief are characteristics which may be taken into account in assessing provocation. In one of the earliest "honour killing" cases reported, this was left unclear.[20] Shabir Hussain had killed his sister-in-law, Tasleem Begum, by running her over with his car and then reversing back over her body. Although the defendant was initially convicted of murder, on appeal the conviction was quashed and at the retrial the prosecution accepted his plea of guilty of manslaughter by reason of provocation. Because of this, the question of objective loss of self-control was not directly tested in court. However, during sentencing the judge accepted that "something blew up in your head that caused you a complete and sudden loss of self control." Although the judge did not explicitly state that the loss of self-control was caused by the adultery of the victim, and the defendant's consequent perception of this as shameful, the preceding statement acknowledged that this "would be deeply offensive to someone with your background and your religious beliefs." He then went on to give a reduced sentence of six-and-a-half years rather than eight years due to "the mitigating factors that have been identified."[21] The fact that the prosecution did not contest his plea of manslaughter on grounds of provocation indicates that it considered that there was sufficient evidence to support the plea. However, the lack of explicit comment on the manner in which the objective limb of the provocation test was satisfied makes it difficult to ascertain whether the defendant's cultural beliefs were taken into account as a characteristic which affected only the gravity of the provocation, or also the level of self-control he was expected to have. Likewise the "mitigating factors" mentioned in setting the sentence could well have included the cultural background referred to earlier. At the very least, the focus on cultural background in the sentencing remarks does show that cultural issues were deemed relevant enough for the court to comment on them in this early case.

The issue of cultural background or belief as a characteristic to be taken into account in assessing the objective element of provocation was examined more directly in the later case of *Faqir Mohammed*.[22] The defendant killed his daughter Shahida after finding a man in her bedroom, and pleaded provocation on the basis that the thought that his daughter had sexual relations outside marriage had so provoked him that he had lost self-control and stabbed her. At the original trial the judge directed the jury to follow the ruling in Smith.[23] Thus, they were directed to examine whether the defendant's cultural and religious beliefs on sex outside marriage and arranged marriage, especially with regard to daughters, should be taken into account in relation not only to the gravity of the provocation, but also the level of self-control he should be expected to exercise. The jury rejected his plea of provocation and found him guilty of murder. His appeal was also rejected; however, the appeal court did rule that *Attorney General for Jersey v Holley*[24] should have been followed instead, so that although the cultural and religious beliefs of the defendant could be taken into account in relation to the assessment of the gravity of the provocation he suffered, they could not be taken into account in assessing whether he had exercised the level of self control expected of a reasonable man in the same circumstances. The judge should instead have directed the jury to consider whether a person of the age and sex of the applicant, and with ordinary self-control, would have acted as the applicant did. This means that cultural characteristics are not to be viewed in the same way as an innate characteristic such as age, which the defendant has no control over. To this extent the courts seem willing to view cultural characteristics as less fixed. However, it is troubling that they can still be used to assess the gravity of the provocation (if not the level of self control), in the same way as impotence, for example, in the earlier case law. Thus, even this aspect of the provocation test to some extent perpetuates a conception of culture as fixed and beyond the control of the defendant, rather than subject to intra-group power hierarchies and contingent on context.[25]

The overarching problems of cultural stereotyping and the disregard of the influence of patriarchal norms in "honour killing" cases go beyond the specific problems found in the provocation test. The judge's summing up in the original trial of Faqir Mohammed[26] accepted evidence on the defendant's cultural background, attitudes to female sexuality, and behaviour towards the victim, which portrayed the Pakistani community in question as homogenous and uniformly restrictive in its attitudes towards sex outside marriage and honour and shame. This view was also referred to in the appeal court judgment. The evidence itself may well have been largely accurate; however, it is troubling that the courts at each stage unquestioningly accepted the evidence of largely male witnesses as to the cultural norms surrounding the defendant's actions. The effect of this is not only to perpetuate ideas of culture (rather than individual deviance) as determinative of the ethnic minority defendant's behaviour, but also to present a male-dominated and static view of the culture under scrutiny. This demonstrates how the use of cultural evidence can be harmful when it attempts to fix or reify culture into a form which can be easily digested within the adversarial legal process. Nuances as to the relative role of culture or gender in a case are thus lost, because of the law's need to categorise and define the culture on which evidence is being introduced.

Cultural issues were referred to in the re-sentencing of Shabir Hussain, and also in the sentencing of Abdulla Younes, after his conviction for the murder of his daughter Heshu. In the latter case the judge made reference in his sentencing remarks to the case as "a tragic story arising out of, to quote defence counsel, irreconcilable cultural difficulties between traditional Kurdish values and the values of Western society."[27] The murders of Heshu Younes, Tasleem Begum and Shahida Mohammed revolved around excessive patriarchal attempts to regulate or control female sexuality. Yet judicial discourse on an alleged "clash of cultures" between ethnic minority and majority communities ignores this aspect and implies the cultural superiority of the majority community, as well as fuelling the stereotyping of minority communities. It fails to highlight the location of such crimes within a wider scheme of patriarchal violence against women, instead marking out a reified version of "culture" as the sole or key factor in the motivation and perpetration of such crimes.

These cases highlight a number of potential problems with the use of cultural evidence in cases of "honour killing." The first is the role of the courts in stereotyping "culture" and portraying it as static and immutable within the context of ethnic minority communities. This reinforces, secondly, the inability of the courts to recognise the importance of cross-cultural gender issues, such as the control of female sexuality, in the perpetration of such violence. Thirdly, this upholds ideas of honour codes as primarily culturally rather than gender-based, which separates honour-related violence from other forms of violence against women on the basis of alleged cultural difference. This in turn hinders attempts to locate honour-related violence within wider gender violence, and to enable rights-based approaches for the protection of women, such as "mature multiculturalism." Fourthly, and importantly, it is not the intention of this article to argue that it is the use of cultural evidence per se that is problematic in cases of honour-related violence, but rather its inappropriate use, in ways that negate women's fundamental rights to be free from gender violence, and that accept male-dominated interpretations of culture instead. This is shown by the contrast between the cases involving male defendants discussed here, and cases involving female defendants such as Zoora Shah.[28] In the latter case, contextualising evidence on the cultural background of the defendant was disregarded by the court, even though it was crucial to understanding what had led her to behave in a certain way, and thus to the success of her appeal. A "mature multiculturalism" approach would perhaps better ensure that the positive aspects of understanding cultural issues are utilised by the courts, at the same time as not allowing them to supersede the right to be free from gender violence, including honour-related violence.

The case law surrounding forced marriages shows somewhat more development in terms of the appropriate admittance of cultural evidence, and highlights further the necessity of not ignoring such evidence where it may help protect victims. The civil courts were at first unreceptive to claims of culture in determining whether duress was present to vitiate consent to marry. Thus, in the early case of *Singh v Singh*,[29] before multiculturalism had become accepted in the UK, the Court of Appeal held that even though the petitioner had acted out of respect for her parents and cultural traditions, the marriage could not be declared void because no immediate or life-threatening danger was present. The Court did not consider more subtle coercion to be relevant to the validity of the consent, such as the fact that the petitioner was only 17 at the time of the marriage, spoke poor English, and would have been disowned by her parents had she refused. This case demonstrates how not admitting cultural evidence in certain circumstances can be as damaging to victims of honour-related violence as admitting it is in other circumstances. Fortunately, this was not followed in the later case of *Hirani v Hirani*,[30] where a decree of nullity was granted to a young Hindu woman who argued that she had only gone through with the arranged marriage because of threats by her parents, upon whom she was financially dependent, to turn her out of their home should she refuse. In the more recent Scottish case of *Mahmood v Mahmood*,[31] the court stated that the particular threats the applicant received were sufficient to overwhelm the will of a girl of her age and cultural background. These cases indicate that the willingness of the courts to acknowledge cultural factors where appropriate when investigating duress, has gradually increased over the decades alongside policies of multiculturalism and cultural diversity.

Alongside this, in the related area of abduction abroad for forced marriage, although still sensitive to cultural factors, the courts have been more aware of gender factors in their approach to protecting victims. The parents of Rehana Bashir were imprisoned for attempting to drug her and take her to Pakistan and marry her without her consent.[32] Most significantly, in the landmark decision in *Re KR*,[33] a 17-year-old Sikh girl abducted by her parents to India for forced marriage was made a ward of the court. In his judgment, Justice Singer made clear that whilst the courts acknowledged the difficulty faced by minorities in attempting to retain their cultural traditions, the usual sensitivity of the courts to the traditional and religious values of minority communities would give way to the integrity of the young person, whose voice would prevail in the context of arranged or enforced marriages. This decision sees culture as a more mutable factor, and unlike the provocation cases discussed above, represents a "mature multiculturalism" approach to honour-based violence, since it is influenced by growing awareness of how to balance the aims of cultural diversity with the protection of victims from gender-based violence. It is to be hoped that the jurisprudence on forced marriages will continue to adopt this more nuanced approach; taking cultural factors into account when appropriate and relevant, but ensuring that they are not allowed to outweigh the rights of victims to be free from gender-based violence. However, it remains to be seen whether such an approach will also be adopted in future cases of "honour killing" involving provocation.

Conclusion

Despite the problems arising from the identification of "honour crimes" as a primarily cultural tradition or practice, and the promising sensitivity of judicial attitudes in certain cases involving "honour," it seems that the law often continues to identify such cases primarily according to cultural criteria. However, elsewhere the law has taken a contradictory position and ignored cultural context, which can also result in injustice to victims of gender violence. Thus the solution is not for the courts to disregard all cultural evidence as a matter of course, but to be sensitive to the circumstances of its introduction in individual cases. As Sen (2005, p. 50) argues, "to posit a specificity that is flawed and that fails to see linkages is problematic; to deny specificity if it exists is also problematic." At the same time, greater focus on the gendered aspects of honour-related violence would place it more firmly within the spectrum of violence against women across all communities in the UK, with less risk of stereotyping and stigmatising ethnic minority communities. As more cases of honour-related violence come to light and are subjected to judicial scrutiny, it is to be hoped that the need to incorporate both gender and cultural factors appropriately into the legal process will become more evident. Until such time, the categorisation of "honour crimes" continues to raise more questions than answers.

Acknowledgements

The author would like to thank Professor Lynn Welchman, Professor Werner Menski, the editors of Feminist Legal Studies and the anonymous referees for their support and helpful comments on drafts of this article. My thanks also to Professor Anne Phillips for allowing me access to the transcripts referred to in the final section.

Footnotes

1. I use quotation marks around the term "honour" in order to convey the fact that I am in agreement with an increasing number of activists and academics critical of its overall utility in distinguishing between types of gender violence. See Welchman and Hossain (2005) for in-depth analysis of this point.

2. A summary of responses to the consultation exercise on the proposed criminalisation of forced marriage is available at http://www.fco.gov.uk/en/fco-in-action/nationals/forced-marriage-unit/fmconsultation.
The Forced Marriage (Civil Protection) Act 2007, which received assent in July 2007 and is to be implemented in Autumn 2008, provides for the making of Forced Marriage Protection Orders (with an attached power of arrest) by the family courts.

3. I would also theorise rape as a type of "honour crime," since it is used as an enforcement mechanism to control behaviour or punish transgressions of "honour" codes, and may also lead to other forms of violence, such as "honour killing" or forced marriage, to remove the perceived stain to male or family "honour." However, the scope of this essay permits only examination of "honour killings" and forced marriage in more detail. See Welchman and Hossain (2005) for a detailed analysis of the issues surrounding the definition of 'honour crimes'.

4. *Mahmud v Mahmud* [1994] SLT 599. There have also been a number of cases of "honour killing" of male victims reported in the press, one example being the 2004 case of Zafar Iqbal in Bradford, who was murdered by his wife's relatives after they married without their approval (see Grattage 2004).

5. Other factors relevant to this aspect of the discussion, which cannot be explored in detail here, are the role of female perpetrators and the intergenerational nature of much honour-related violence. However, the writing of Kandiyoti (1988) on 'patriarchal bargaining' is potentially of great help in analysing both of these aspects of honour-related violence.

6. See Safra Project (2002) for a more detailed analysis of how "honour" affects Muslim lesbian, bisexual and transgender women in accessing social and legal services in the UK.

7. Whilst I am unaware of reported cases of "honour killings" on the basis of sexual orientation to date in the UK, the recently reported murder of young gay man Ahmet Yildiz in Turkey is suspected to have been an "honour killing" motivated by the victim's outspoken work as a gay rights activis (see Birch 2008).

8. As An-Na'im (2005, pp. 67–68) argues, all societies regulate sexuality to some extent, and attempts to argue that families and communities should have no right to do so may be counterproductive, since this may result in increased risks to victims as attempts are made to ensure even tighter regulation of sexuality. Thus, it is not the regulation of sexuality in itself which is problematic, but rather the excessive or discriminatory regulation of sexuality.

9. Council of Europe Parliamentary Assembly, Resolution 1327: So-called "honour crimes"'(4 April 2003).

10. See also Razack (2004) for detailed discussion of these points in the Norwegian context, in relation to policy on immigration and forced marriages.

11. See Phillips (2007) for a detailed and convincing argument that multiculturalism can be reconciled with gender equality if it moves beyond essentialist notions of culture.

12. For this reason the "balancing" or "proportionality" principle in human rights law is not strictly relevant here, since in the UK there is no direct claim being made by perpetrators of honour-related violence that they should have a "right" to commit "honour killings," for example, in response to a perceived transgression by the victim. Rather, it is that for a number of reasons they are unwilling to accept that where they do so, the state should be able to take action to punish them, and the severity of that punishment.

13. Since this discussion is restricted to the UK context, I do not engage with the broader debate around universalism and cultural relativism. However, see Coomaraswamy (2005b), Afkhami (1999), Steiner and Alston (1996, Chap. 4), Rao (1995) and Bunting (1993) for exploration of the international human rights dimensions of the debate.

14. The HRA implements the European Convention on Human Rights (ECHR) in UK law. "Honour crimes" such as "honour killing" and forced marriage may violate a number of articles of the ECHR, including Article 2 (the right to life), Article 3 (freedom from torture or inhuman or degrading treatment or punishment), Article 5 (the right to liberty and security of the person), Article 8 (the right to respect for private and family life), Article 12 (the right to marry and form a family), and Article 14 (non-dis- crimination in the enjoyment of the foregoing rights and freedoms).

15. In effect, this is an "indirect horizontal obligation" dependent on recognising that state authorities have failed in their duties to an individual by not adequately protecting or preventing a violation of their rights by another private individual. See *Osman v UK* (2000) 29 EHRR 245 and *X & Y v Netherlands* (1986) 8 EHRR 235 as key cases which establish this principle in European human rights jurisprudence. For more general commentary and case law on this issue, see Emmerson et al. (2007, Chap. 18), Fenwick (2007, p. 249), Stone (2006, p. 38), Starmer et al. (2001, p. 151).

16. For more detailed arguments as to why and how positive or horizontal obligations come into effect in relation to domestic violence in the UK, including case law, see Choudhry and Herring (2006a, b).

17. Although it is not possible to re-state the law on provocation in greater detail here, Clarkson et al. (2007, pp. 714–723) and Ormerod (2008, pp. 585–617) provide further reading on texts and case law on both the objective and subjective requirements of the legal test for provocation.

18. *R v Bedder* [1954] 1 WLR 1119.

19. *DPP v Camplin* [1978] AC 705.

20. *R v Shabir Hussain* [1997] EWCA Crim 24.

21. *R v Shabir Hussain*, Newcastle Crown Court, 28 July 1998.

22. *R v Faqir Mohammed* [2005] EWCA Crim 1880.

23. *R v Smith (Morgan)* [2001] 1 AC 1. This case ruled that certain characteristics of the defendant, in this instance depression, could be taken into account in assessing both the gravity of the provocation and the level of self-control expected. However, this was overturned by the Privy Council *in Attorney General for Jersey v Holley* [2005] 2 AC 580, which returned the test to the earlier, pre-*Smith* position that characteristics other than age and sex could only be taken into account in relation to the gravity of the provocation and not in relation to the expected level of self-control. The decision in Jersey has since

been followed in a number of cases including *Faqir Mohammed*. See Clarkson et al. (2007, pp. 732–734).

24. [2005] 2 AC 580.

25. The government is currently attempting to address critiques of the provocation defence as lacking in gender sensitivity. Under proposed reforms, sexual infidelity would no longer be relevant to establishing provocation, in order to prevent men who kill for this reason taking advantage of the defence. Conversely, fear of serious violence, or words or conduct which leave the defendant feeling justifiably wronged, would be taken into account, allowing women who kill as a result of domestic violence to take better advantage of the defence than is currently the case (see Pallister and Stevenson 2008). However, it is likely that whatever changes are ultimately made to this area of law, there will still be scope for judicial interpretation of the relevance of "culture," and thus, potentially, for continuing problems of the type discussed here.

26. *R v Faqir Mohammed*, Manchester Crown Court, 18 February 2002.

27. *R v. Abdulla M. Younes*, Central Criminal Court, 29 September 2003. This was the first case the Metropolitan Police labelled as an "honour killing," according to Southall Black Sisters (see Siddiqui 2005, p. 269).

28. *R v Zoora Ghulam Shah*, Court of Appeal, Criminal Division, 30 April 1998. See Phillips (2003, p. 524) and Patel (2003, p. 243) for discussion of this case, and of the crucial involvement of Southall Black Sisters in her appeal. Shah had left an abusive husband and was taken in by a drug dealer who proceeded to abuse her and prostitute her to his friends. When he began to show interest in her daughter, she put arsenic powder in his food in an attempt to dampen his libido, culminating in an overdose. At the initial trial Shah did not give evidence on these issues and was found guilty of murder. When she gave evidence of the abuse at her appeal, the court refused to entertain the idea that she had not done so at the initial trial for reasons of "honour" and a fear of shaming herself and her daughters further in the community. In their view, the experiences she described were such that it was not conceivable that she in fact had any "honour" left to salvage.

29. [1971] 2 All ER 828.

30. [1983] 4 FLR 232.

31. [1993] SLT 589.

32. *Sakina Bibi Khan and Mohammed Bashir* [1999] 1 Cr App R (S) 329.

33. *Re KR (a child) (abduction: forcible removal by parents)* [1999] 4 All ER 954.

References

Abu-Odeh, Lama. 1996. Crimes of honour and the construction of gender in Arab societies. In *Feminism and Islam*, ed. Mai Yamani, 141–193. Reading: Ithaca Press.

Afkhami, Mahnaz. 1999. Cultural relativism and women's human rights. In *Women and international human rights law, Vol. II: International courts, instruments and select regional issues affecting women*, ed. Kelly D. Askin and Dorean M. Koenig, 479–486. New York: Transnational Publishers Inc.

An-Na'im, Abdullahi Ahmed. 2000. Forced marriage. http://www.soas.ac.uk/honourcrimes/FMpaper AnNa'im.htm. Accessed 15 September 2008.

An-Na'im, Abdullahi Ahmed. 2005. The role of "community discourse" in combating "crimes of honour": Preliminary assessment and prospects. In *"Honour": Crimes, paradigms and violence against women*, ed. Lynn Welchman and Sara Hossain, 64–77. London: Zed Books.

Araji, Sharon K. 2000. Crimes of honour and shame: Violence against women in non- Western and Western societies. *The red feather journal of postmodern criminology*, http://www.critcrim. org/ redfeather/journal-pomocrim/vol-8-shaming/araji.html. Accessed 15 September 2008.

Baker, Nancy V., Peter R. Gregware, and Margery A. Cassidy. 1999. Family killing fields: Honor rationales in the murder of women. *Violence Against Women* 5: 164–184.

Ballard, Roger. 1994. Introduction: The emergence of Desh Pardesh. In *Desh Pardesh: The south Asian presence in Britain*, ed. Roger Ballard, 1–34. London: C. Hurst.

Bashar, Nazife. 1983. Rape in England between 1550 and 1700. In *Men's power, women's resistance: The sexual dynamics of history*, ed. London Feminist History Group, 29–42. London: Pluto Press.

Bauer, Jan, and Anissa Helie. 2006. *Documenting women's rights violations by non-state actors: Activist strategies from Muslim communities*. Canada: International Centre for Human Rights and Democratic Development and Women Living Under Muslim Laws.

Bhavnani, Kum-Kum. 1993. Towards a multicultural Europe? "Race," nation and identity in 1992 and beyond. *Feminist Review* 45: 30–45.

Birch, Nicholas. 2008. Was Ahmet Yildiz the victim of Turkey's first gay honour killing? *The Independent*, 19 July.

Bulmer, Martin, and John Solomos. 1998. Introduction: Re-thinking ethnic and racial studies. *Ethnic and Racial Studies* 21: 819–837.

Bunting, Annie. 1993. Theorizing women's cultural diversity in feminist international human rights strategies. *Journal of Law and Society* 20: 6–22.

Chakravarti, Uma. 2005. From fathers to husbands: Of love, death and marriage in north India. In *"Honour": Crimes, paradigms and violence against women*, ed. Lynn Welchman and Sara Hossain, 308–331. London: Zed Books.

Choudhry, Shazia, and Jonathan Herring. 2006a. Righting domestic violence. *International Journal of Law, Policy and the Family* 20: 95–119.

Choudhry, Shazia, and Jonathan Herring. 2006b. Domestic violence and the Human Rights Act 1998: A new means of legal intervention? *Public Law* 2006: 752–784.

Clark, Anna. 1983. Rape or seduction? A controversy over sexual violence in the nineteenth century. *In Men's power, women's resistance: The sexual dynamics of history*, ed. London Feminist History Group, 13–27. London: Pluto Press.

Clark, Anna. 1989. Whores and gossips: Sexual reputation in London 1170–1825. In *Current issues in women's history*, ed. Anna Angerman, 231–248. London: Routledge.

Clarkson, Christopher M.V., Heather M. Keating, and Sally R. Cunningham. 2007. *Clarkson and Keating criminal law: Text and materials*, 6th ed. London: Sweet and Maxwell.

Cohen, Joshua, Matthew Howard, and Martha C. Nussbaum. 1999. Introduction: Feminism, multicul- turalism and human equality. In *Is multiculturalism bad for women? Susan Moller Okin with respondents*, ed. Joshua Cohen, Matthew Howard, and Martha C. Nussbaum, 3–5. Princeton: Princeton University Press.

Coomaraswamy, Radhika. 2005a. Violence against women and 'crimes of honour'. In *"Honour": Crimes, paradigms and violence against women*, ed. Lynn Welchman and Sara Hossain, xi–xiv. London: Zed Books.

Coomaraswamy, Radhika. 2005b. Identity within: Cultural relativism, minority rights and the empowerment of women. In *Men's laws, women's lives*, ed. Indira Jaising, 23–55. New Delhi: Women Unlimited.

Emmerson, Ben, Andrew Ashworth, and Alison Macdonald. 2007. *Human rights and criminal justice*, 2nd ed. London: Sweet and Maxwell.

Fenwick, Helen. 2007. *Civil liberties and human rights*, 4th ed. Abingdon: Routledge Cavendish.

Gilmore, David D. 1987. Introduction: The shame of dishonour. In *Honour and shame in the unity of the Mediterranean*, ed. David D. Gilmore, 2–21. Washington, DC: American Anthropological Association.

Goksel, Iklim. 2006. Virginity and masculinity. In *Men of the global south: A reader*, ed. Adam Jones, 55–58. London: Zed Books.

Grattage, Karen. 2004. Cousins jailed for plotting to kill newlywed. *The Guardian*, 10 November.

Harris, Ruth. 1989. *Murders and madness: Medicine, law and society in the fin de sie`cle*. Oxford: Clarendon Press.

Hassan, Yasmeen. 1999. Stove burning, acid throwing and honor killings. In *Women and International human rights law, Vol. II: International courts, instruments and select regional issues affecting women*, ed. Kelly D. Askin and Dorean M. Koenig, 587–

611. New York: Transnational Publishers Inc.

Hellgren, Zenia, and Barbara Hobson. 2006. Intercultural dialogues in the good society: The case of honor killings in Sweden. Paper presented at the Gender Equality, Cultural Diversity: European Comparisons Conference, Free University, Amsterdam, 8–9 June.

Kandiyoti, Deniz. 1988. Bargaining with patriarchy. *Gender and Society* 2: 274 290.

Lindisfarne, Nancy. 1994. Variant masculinities, variant virginities: Rethinking "honour and shame." *In Dislocating masculinity: Comparative ethnographies*, ed. Andrea Cornwall and Nancy Lindisfarne, 82–96. London: Routledge.

Okin, Susan M. 1999. Is multiculturalism bad for women? *In Is multiculturalism bad for women? Susan Moller Okin with respondents*, ed. Joshua Cohen, Matthew Howard, and Martha C. Nussbaum, 7–24. Princeton: Princeton University Press.

Ormerod, David. 2008. *Smith and Hogan criminal law: Cases and materials*, 9th ed. Oxford: Oxford University Press.

Pallister, David, and Rachel Stevenson. 2008. Plans to reform murder laws unveiled. *The Guardian*, 29 July.

Patel, Pragna. 2000. Gender and racial discrimination: An urgent need to integrate an Intersectional perspective to the examination and development of policies, strategies and remedies for gender and racial equality. Paper presented at the

UNDAW Expert Group Meeting on the Gender-Related Aspects of Race Discrimination, Zagreb, Croatia, 21–24 November. http://www.un.org/womeneatch/daw/csw/Patel45.htm. Accessed 15 September 2008.

Patel, Pragna. 2003. Shifting Terrains: Old Struggles For New? In

From homebreakers to jailbreakers: Southall black sisters, ed. Rahila Gupta, 234–260. London: Zed Books.

Patel, Pragna. 2008. Faith in the state? Asian women's struggles for human rights in the UK. *Feminist Legal Studies* 16: 9–36.

Phillips, Anne. 2003. When culture means gender: Issues of cultural defence in the English courts. *Modern Law Review* 66: 510–531.

Phillips, Anne. 2007. *Multiculturalism without culture*. Princeton: Princeton University Press.

Pollit, Katha. 1999. Whose culture? In *Is multiculturalism bad for women?* Susan Moller Okin with respondents, ed. Joshua Cohen, Matthew Howard, and Martha C. Nussbaum, 27–30. Princeton: Princeton University Press.

Prins, Baukje, and Sawitri Saharso. 2006. Cultural diversity, gender equality: The Dutch case. Paper presented at the Gender Equality, Cultural Diversity: European Comparisons Conference, Free University, Amsterdam, 8–9 June.

Rao, Arati. 1995. The politics of gender and culture in international human rights discourse. In *Women's rights, human rights: International feminist perspectives*, ed. Julie Peters and Andrea Wolper, 167–175. London: Routledge.

Razack, Sherene. 2004. Imperilled Muslim women, dangerous Muslim men and civilised Europeans: Legal and social responses to forced marriages. *Feminist Legal Studies* 12: 129–174.

Safra Project. 2002. Identifying the difficulties experienced by Muslim lesbian, bisexual and transgender women in accessing social and legal services. http://www.safraproject.org/Reports/Safra_Project-Initial_findings–2002.pdf. Accessed 15 September 2008.

Sen, Purna. 2005. "Crimes of honour": Value and meaning. In *'Honour': Crimes, paradigms and violence against women*, ed. Lynn Welchman and Sara Hossain, 42–63. London: Zed Books.

Shachar, Ayelet. 2001. *Multicultural jurisdictions: Cultural differences and women's rights*. Cambridge: Cambridge University Press.

Siddiqui, Hannana. 2000. The ties that bind. *Index on censorship* 1: 50–53.

Siddiqui, Hannana. 2003. "It was written in her kismet": Forced marriage. *In From homebreakers to jailbreakers: Southall Black Sisters*, ed. Rahila Gupta, 67–91. London: Zed Books.

Siddiqui, Hannana. 2005. "There is no 'honour' in domestic violence, only shame!" Women's struggles against "honour" crimes in the UK. In *"Honour": Crimes, paradigms and violence against women*, ed. Lynn Welchman and Sara Hossain, 263–281. London: Zed Books.

Spierenburg, Peter. 1998. *Men and violence: Gender, honor and rituals in modern Europe and America.* Columbus, OH: Ohio State University Press.

Starmer, Keir, Francesca Klug, and Ian Byrne. 2001. *Blackstone's human rights digest.* London: Blackstone Press.

Steiner, Henry J., and Philip Alston. 1996. *International human rights in context: Law, politics and morals.* Oxford: Clarendon Press.

Stone, Richard. 2006. *Textbook on civil liberties and human rights*, 6th ed. Oxford: Oxford University Press.

Tamir, Yael. 1999. Siding with the underdogs. In *Is multiculturalism bad for women?*

Susan Moller Okin with respondents, ed. Joshua Cohen, Matthew Howard, and Martha C. Nussbaum, 47–52. Princeton: Princeton University Press.

Touma-Sliman, Aida. 2005. Culture, national minority and the state: Working against the crime of "family honour" within the Palestinian community in Israel. In *"Honour": Crimes, paradigms and violence against women*, ed. Lynn Welchman and Sara Hossain, 181–198. London: Zed Books.

Volpp, Leti. 2001. Feminism versus multiculturalism. *Columbia Law Review* 101: 1181–1218.

Welchman, Lynn, and Sara Hossain. 2005. "Honour": Rights and wrongs. In *"Honour": Crimes, paradigms and violence against women*, ed. Lynn Welchman and Sara Hossain, 1–21. London: Zed Books.

Women Against Fundamentalism, and Southall Black Sisters. 2007. Joint submission to the Commission on Integration and Cohesion. http://waf.gn.apc.org/documents/WAF_SBS_report.doc. Accessed 15 September 2008.

Periodical and Internet Sources Bibliography

The following articles have been selected to supplement the diverse views presented in this chapter.

Aneela Batool. "Same story, different ending," *Maclean's,* vol. 123, issue 35, September 13, 2010, pp. 70-71.

Stella Dawson. "Two girls murdered in Texas taxi: Were they honor killings?" *Reuters U.S.,* June 18, 2015. http://www.reuters.com/article/us-violence-women-honourkillings-idUSKBN0OY2UK20150618.

Fadia Faqir. "Intrafamily femicide in defence of honour: the case of Jordan," *Third World Quarterly,* vol. 22, issue 1, February, 2001, pp. 65-82.

Michael Friscolanti. "TAINTED VERDICT," *Maclean's,* vol. 128, issue 42, October 26, 2015, pp. 36-37.

Michelle Goldberg. "MARRY—OR ELSE," *Newsweek,* vol. 158, issue 13, September 26, 2011, pp. 48-51.

Sunny Hundal. "No silence over honour killings," *New Statesman*, vol. 141, issue 5118, August 13, 2012, pp. 15-15.

Abigail Pesta. "An American Tragedy," *Marie Claire (US Edition),* vol. 17, issue 8, August 2010, pp. 98-188.

Jihan Thompson. "DISPATCH: Honor Killings Come Stateside," *Marie Claire (US Edition),* vol. 15, issue 11, November 2008, pp. 82-83.

GLOBALVIEWPOINTS

CHAPTER 4

What Can Be Done About Honor Killing?

What Must the United States Do to Stop Honor Killing?

Elaine McCartin

In the following viewpoint, Elaine McCartin, who specializes in communications, identifies several factors behind individual cases of honor killing being reported. She argues that, although some use Islam to justify such violence, documented condemnation by Muslim clerics and devout religious practitioners has occurred. McCartin contends that the United States has the power to alleviate this suffering for women.

As you read, consider the following questions:

1. According to McCartin, what must the US Congress do to prevent violence against women?
2. As defined, how does impunity contribute to the escalation of honor killing?
3. Which two groups have condemned misinterpretation of Islam to justify honor violence?

On May 27, a 25 year-old pregnant woman named Farzana Parveen was stoned to death by her father, brother, ex-fiancé, and about a dozen other men.

Her crime? Marrying the man she loved instead of her cousin, a coupling that her father had arranged years before.

Farzana's husband, Mohammad Iqbal, the man her family did

"What are 'Honor Killings' and How Can We Make Them Stop?" by Elaine McCartin, Women Thrive Worldwide, June 4, 2014. Reprinted by permission.

not approve of, is not without blame. Six years ago, Mohammad killed his first wife so that he could marry Farzana. Mohammad casually admitted his past action in an interview just last week with CNN:

> *"I wanted to send a proposal to Farzana so I killed my wife."*

Mohammad was arrested but later released because his son forgave him. Under Pakistani law, family members of honor killing victims can forgive and pardon the culprits.

Mohammad's blasé admission of killing his first wife exemplifies the apathetic attitudes that often surround violence against women.

Farzana's husband's previous crime does not make her honor killing any less wrong or significant. What happened to Farzana is a tragedy, and the attitudes and behaviors surrounding women and their freedom to choose who and when they want to marry must change, as should attitudes around acceptable violence against women.

What is an "Honor Killing?"

According to the Honor Based Violence Awareness Network, an "honor" killing is the most extreme form of honor-based violence.

Honor-based violence is characterized as "a phenomenon where a person (most often a woman) is subjected to violence by her collective family or community in order to restore 'honor', presumed to have been lost by her behavior, most often through expressions of sexual autonomy."

According to a spokesman for Women Living Under Muslim Law:

> *"[An honor killing is] a form of torturing someone to death. It is one of the most brutal forms of violence perpetrated against women in order to control and punish their sexuality and basic freedoms."*

Not an Isolated Case

Farzana's story has captured the media's attention and sparked outrage around the world, but her case is not unique.

In Pakistan alone, rights groups estimate that nearly 1,000 women die *in honor killings each year.*

Honor killings are not limited to the Middle East. The United Nations estimates that 5,000 women worldwide are victims of honor killings each year. However, honor killings often go unreported, so women's advocacy groups say the figure could be as high as 20,000 a year.

In one particularly tragic case, a 13 year-old girl in Somalia was killed after claiming that three men had raped her. She reported the crime to authorities, but there was no investigation. Instead, she was charged with adultery. She was taken to a stadium where she was buried up to her neck and stoned to death by 50 men while 1,000 people watched.

Such violence often silences women who have been raped or suffered some other horrific attack that, in many places, is blamed on the woman. They may fear further repercussions by family members who see their violation as a dishonor to the family's good name.

What is the Role of Islam in Honor Killings?

Perpetrators of honor killings and honor-based violence often use Islamic teachings as a justification for their actions. But clerics and devout Muslims worldwide have condemned this misinterpretation. Honor killings are murders, and perpetrators should be punished to the fullest extent of the law.

Why Do Honor Killings Still Happen?

The reason behind the persistence of honor killings is rooted in sexual inequality. Rothna Begun of Human Rights Watch says that "most 'honor' crimes can be traced to inflexible and discriminatory attitudes about women's roles, especially around sexuality."

Impunity is another key factor that contributes to the proliferation of honor killings. "Since almost no one is tried and convicted for such killings, rights groups say it is no surprise that 'honor crimes' are on the rise in Pakistan."

When culprits are arrested, they are usually freed due to intentionally flawed police investigations or they are forgiven and pardoned by the victim's relatives, as was the case with Farzana's husband.

What Can the U.S. Do to Stop Honor Killings?

The United States Congress must pass the International Violence Against Women Act. This bill, which was introduced in the House of Representatives in 2013 and in the Senate this May, would ensure that U.S. foreign policy includes comprehensive strategies to prevent and respond to violence against women and girls, including honor killings.

What Can You Do Right Now?

You can make an immediate impact by submitting a photo to the No1Nowhere campaign. By submitting a photo you are telling the world that no one should be subjected to gender-based violence, and nowhere should women and girls have to live in fear of sexual or physical violence.

The No1Nowhere campaign sends a public message about just how many people in the around the globe want to end honor killings and all violence against women and girls once and for all.

Jordan Needs to Implement a Safety Net for Women

Equality Now

In the following viewpoint, Equality Now maintains that the legal framework in Jordan must change and reflect a stance against condoning honor killings. Additionally, women who face violence often have nowhere to shelter except in state-run women's prisons. Equality Now, which seeks to use the law to protect and promote the rights of women and girls, offers directives to apply pressure by writing the minister of social development in Jordan to fulfill commitments to protect all of Jordan's citizens.

As you read, consider the following questions:

1. What benefits do perpetrators receive from articles 97 and 98 of Jordan's penal codes?
2. Where do Jordanian women go when threatened with violence?
3. What types of services could women expect at a government-sponsored shelter?

In January 2002, two brothers from Jordan were given a three-month prison sentence for killing their sister Safa Samir on 7 July 2001. When Safa returned to her home on 6 July she confessed to her family that she had engaged in sexual activity with a man. That day her brother Anas Samir tried to kill her with an axe in

"Jordan: National Efforts to Confront "Honor Killings" and to Protect Women from Violence," equalitynow.org. Reprinted by permission.

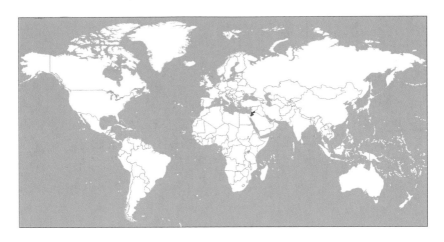

the backyard of the family's home. Safa was admitted briefly to the hospital. The following day Anas reportedly told his younger brother Musa that they must kill their sister because "he could not stand people's looks or comments that their sister was not a pure woman." The brothers went to her room, tied a rope around her neck, and each of them pulled one end. When this did not kill her, they fetched a garden hose and squeezed it tightly around her neck until she suffocated to death. The brothers then turned themselves in to the police, claiming to have killed their sister to cleanse the family's honor. They were tried for premeditated murder, but the Criminal Court reduced the charge to a misdemeanor citing Article 98 of the Penal Code, which stipulates that a person "provoked" into committing a crime benefits from a reduction in penalty. "The two defendants benefit from a reduction in penalty because their sister's acts brought shame to her family," the court ruled.

Another nearly two dozen women and children have been killed in Jordan so far in 2002 in the name of family honor. The legitimacy of such crimes is rooted in a complex code of honor sanctioned by tradition and social customs, whereby a male relative must kill a woman to restore the family's good name in the community where the woman's virtue has come into question. Women may be killed by a family member for violating sexual norms, or for being victims of rape, incest, sexual abuse or sexual rumor. The United Nations reports that such killings have also occurred in Bangladesh, Brazil, Ecuador, Egypt, India, Israel, Italy, Morocco, Norway, Pakistan, Peru, Sweden, Turkey, Uganda, the United Kingdom and Venezuela. Other countries, too, are being investigated for reports of "honor" killings.

In December 2000, Equality Now issued a Women's Action on the issue of "honor" killings in Jordan calling for a change in the legislation that would abolish the legal framework that condoned the practice. In December 2001, Article 340 of the Penal Code, which exempted from punishment men who kill their wives or female relatives found committing adultery, was repealed and replaced with a provision that permits a reduction in penalty only if the murder is committed immediately on finding the victim in the act of committing adultery or "in an unlawful bed." While the amendment of Article 340 is welcomed, those committing so-called "honor" killings still benefit from the provisions of Articles 97 and 98, which allow for a reduction in sentence for those who commit a crime in a fit of fury. These Articles are still applied in cases relating to "honor" irrespective of whether the killing was planned, such as in the case of the Samir brothers who clearly premeditated the murder of their sister. Those convicted have traditionally been given very light sentences, generally ranging from between three months to one year in jail. In October 2002, for the first time, the Court of Cassation sent an "honor" crime case back to the Criminal Court for tougher sentencing on the basis that the murder was premeditated. The original 3-month sentence passed against Fawaz Syouf was increased to 10 years. The same Criminal Court however had the previous day handed down a 1-month sentence to a man who beat his sister to death in the name of "honor" and reduced charges to a misdemeanor for a man accused of attempting to poison his 12-year old sister for the sake of "honor."

Women such as these have nowhere to turn when they are under threat of an attack. There is no national women's shelter in Jordan, only state-run women's prisons where women are incarcerated for their own safety. Ironically, their release can only be secured by a male relative. At present a number of women spend indefinite periods of time in prison for their own protection. Major Ibtisam Dhmour, former director of the only women's correctional facility in Jordan, has said that women may be in prison for becoming pregnant out of wedlock or allegedly being involved in an extramarital affair. Others are victims of rape or incest. Experts stress the need for a national women's shelter that would provide immediate refuge for such women.

In response to letters generated by Equality Now's December 2000 Women's Action, former Minister of Social Development Tamam El-Ghul, in a letter dated 7 January 2001, stated her commitment to ensuring the right to life and security of each person and said that a "government-sponsored shelter for women will soon be functioning since all the necessary procedures have been taken with the involvement of both governmental and non-governmental organizations and even concerned UN agencies. Thus women who are under threat or at risk of being killed will be provided with refuge and adequate support services. They will have access to legal and psychological counseling, training and rehabilitation opportunities within the confines of a modern shelter facility." Nearly two years later there are reports that the first national women's shelter will open within six months, although talks appear still to be underway between the Family Protection Department and officials from the Ministry of Social Development to "coordinate efforts and achieve the common goal of establishing a women's shelter." In five days alone at the beginning of September 2002 three women were killed by their male relatives in the name of honor. The youngest, 17-year old Afaf Younes, was shot dead by her father despite his written promise to the authorities not to harm her. She had repeatedly run away from home to protect herself from his alleged sexual abuse of her and had only just recovered from his previous murder attempt. Reports suggest he

There is No Honour in Honour Killing

Islamabad, Pakistan—Prime Minster of Pakistan Nawaz Sharif has re-affirmed the Government of Pakistan's commitment to end discrimination and violence against women and girls, and more so end the menace of honour killings prevalent in Pakistan.

Addressing Pakistan's first screening of Sharmeen Obaid-Chinoy's second Oscar nomination, *A Girl in the River: The Price of Forgiveness*, the Prime Minister of Pakistan in a personal and bold initiative to further strengthen and enhance legislation to work for women said: "There is no honour in honour killing—in fact there can be nothing more brutal than engaging in killing and calling it honour."

In tackling difficult and challenging themes, Sharmeen's second Oscar nomination has captured the personal attention of the Prime Minister of Pakistan with a pledge to build on the momentum from her documentary to take all appropriate steps to end all forms of discrimination and violence against women, and bring perpetrators to justice.

Speaking at the screening, Sharmeen said: "The message of this film is strong and democratically elected representatives are listening to the message of this film and acting on it—This is the biggest win for me."

UN Women Executive Director Phumzile Mlambo-Ngcuka praised the film and the swift political response. "I couldn't agree more with the Prime Minister that there is no honour in honour killings," she said. "UN Women welcomes the Prime Minister's leadership and stands ready to support him and the government to end the practice of killing women in the name of honour."

Country Representative of UN Women in Pakistan Jamshed Kazi lauded the social themes of Sharmeen's inspirational documentaries, saying: "In using film-making as a tool to tackle the long struggle for the rights of women in Pakistan, Sharmeen has contributed to rapidly accelerating the pace of change in society—commitment by the Honourable Prime Minister of Pakistan over the last few days, and today, to end 'honour' killings is a testament to the Government's resolve to strengthen gender justice."

The screening, held on Monday 22 February 2016 at the Prime Ministers House in Islamabad, was attended by government officials, development partners including the UN and civil society representatives.

> The Prime Minster of Pakistan's commitment today to end gender-based discrimination and violence follows adoption along with other world leaders, in September 2015 of a new development framework including a stand-alone sustainable development goal on gender equality and the empowerment of women and girls, as well as gender sensitive targets within the other goals.
>
> —"There is No Honour in Honour Killing: the Prime Minister of Pakistan," by Faria Salman, UN Women, February 23, 2016.

claimed to kill her in the name of honor to cover up his alleged assault. Girls and women continue to die in Jordan without a safe haven to protect them from "honor" crimes.

In June 2000 at the Beijing + 5 Special Session of the United Nations General Assembly, Jordan made a commitment "to develop, adopt and fully implement laws and other measures as appropriate... to eradicate harmful customary or traditional practices including... so-called honor crimes that are violations of the human rights of women and girls..." Jordan is also a party to the Convention on the Elimination of All Forms of Discrimination Against Women and the International Covenant on Civil and Political Rights, both of which proscribe discrimination based on sex.

Please write to the Minister of Social Development, reminding her of the Jordanian government's commitment to protect the right to life and security of all its people and of the previous Minister's pledge to open a national women's shelter. Commend discussions held to date and the positive steps the government has taken to combat domestic violence, in particular under the auspices of the Family Protection Project. Urge her to support women under threat of violence and at risk of being killed by acting immediately to open shelters for women in Jordan.

Please also write to the Minister of Justice, welcoming the amendment of Article 340 and the recent decision of the Court of Cassation in the case of Fawaz Syouf, but noting with concern the continuing practice of "honor" killings and the way in which

Articles 97 and 98 are used to mitigate punishment for these killings. Ask him to take steps to ensure that judges apply the law appropriately and do not use Articles 97 and 98, or Article 340, to allow the justification of "honor" killings. Request him to ensure the courts hold those who commit "honor" crimes properly accountable and that sentences handed down reflect the severity of the crime.

Stop Calling It "Honor" Killing

Cherise Charleswell

In the following viewpoint, Wombanist Views *radio show host and producer Cherise Charleswell argues that violence, including murder, against women as a punishment for supposed immoral behavior should not be referred to as honor killing. Charleswell, women's issues chair at the Hampton Institute, claims that there is nothing honorable about premeditated, brutal murder. She contends that language used to talk about violence against women is based in patriarchy and masculine fragility which automatically assigns blame to the victim and not the aggressor.*

As you read, consider the following questions:

1. What does Charleswell think honor killing should be renamed?
2. According to the author, what are the consequences of fragile masculinity?
3. What is the most critical problem of honor killing?

The term "honor killing" is used to describe an act of murder against a relative, usually a girl or woman, who is perceived to have brought dishonor to the family's reputation by engaging in what is deemed an "immoral" act within their given culture or society. In this respect, they can be looked at as a form of domestic

"There is No "Honor" In Killing: The Problematic Language Used To Describe Violence Against Women," by Cherise Charleswell-Women's Issues Chair, The Hampton Institute, July 26, 2016. Reprinted by permission.

violence, one that is colluded and facilitated, not only by a family, but also the external members of the same community; patriarchal views are used to justify these murders. Also, in many cases, these murders are carried out based on rumors and unfounded suspicions, which resemble witch hunts. It is believed that the only way to restore the family's "honor" is through murder—or punishment by death. These "honor" killings have been carried out by fathers, brothers, and cousins; and female relatives, including mothers—out of fear and/or cultural indoctrination—often are complacent and remain silent about these murders. Even worse is the complacency of society, in that these murders often go unpunished. There are no arrests or trials carried out to seek justice for the deceased. Instead, it seems that the social norms justify the murders—finding the women guilty of inappropriate behavior and thus deserving of capital punishment.

Currently the practice is most commonly associated with regions (and cultures) in North Africa and the Middle East, and with those in the Islamic faith; however, these acts pre-date Islam, and have been carried out in other regions of the world. The practice has a long history, and this likely has much to do with the fact that women and girls, for many centuries, have been subjugated and treated as nothing more than property. It was carried out in the ancient world, including ancient Rome, where the *pater familias*, the senior male of a household, was afforded a number of rights that were not extended to Roman women, including the right kill a daughter or other female relative engaged in pre-marital sex, or a wife having extra-marital relations (Goldstein, 2002). In fact, the Roman law justified homicide "when committed in defense of the chastity either of oneself or relations." (Blackstone, 1966). The Hammurabi Code of the Babylonian civilization had a number of rules that pertained to adultery, and among these rules was that an adulterous wife must be tied to her lover and thrown in the river to drown. The specific text is as follows for laws 132 and 133:

> [132] If the "finger is pointed" at a man's wife about another man, but she is not caught sleeping with the other man, she

shall jump into the river for her husband.

[133] If a man is taken prisoner in war, and there is a sustenance in his house, but his wife leave house and court, and go to another house: because this wife did not keep her court, and went to another house, she shall be judicially condemned and thrown into the water.

While ancient civilizations in the Americas, such as the Aztec and Incas, allowed their own form of "honor" killings: Inca laws allowed husbands to starve their wives if they were suspected of adultery, while Aztec laws permitted stoning or strangulation as punishment for adultery (Goldstein, 2002). Honor-based murders were also codified and practiced in medieval Europe, where early Jewish law mandated death by stoning for an adulterous wife and her partner (Brundage, 1987). Catherine Howard, the fifth wife of England's King Henry VIII, was beheaded based on allegations of adultery, as was the fictitious character Desdemona, in Shakespeare's play, *Othello*.

Women's roles, and increased independence, sexual liberation, etc., did not begin to take root until the 19th century, and was not advanced until the latter half of the 20th century. For many women in the world, these things have not yet been achieved, and the persistence of "honor" killings is an example to this. The following are some of the recent and brutal murders that have been described as "honor" killings:

- The killing of a 26-years-old Pakistani social media star and model Fauzia Akeem, known as Qandeel Baloch, by her brother in the name of preserving their family's honor. Fauna challenged social norms with her glamorous photos and videos that she posted on social media on sites such as Instagram. Reports about her death stated that she was strangled and/or subjected to things that were far more sinister.

- The case of Mohammad Shafia an Afghani man residing in Ontario, Canada, who murdered his three daughters, Zainab 19, Sahar 17, and Geeti 13, after he deemed them to be treacherous. Shafia's anger stemmed from the fact that he felt ashamed that his eldest daughter married a Pakastani man, and he reportedly stated the following when speaking about his daughter's deaths, "I would do it again 100 times,"

- The 2008 movie, *The Stoning of Soraya M.*, is based on the true story of an Iranian woman who was falsely accused of infidelity by her husband, because she refused his request for divorce so that he could marry a 14-years-old girl, only to be ostracized by her community, rejected by her sons, and ultimately sentenced to death by stoning. Soraya was subjected to beatings by her husband before he began the plot against her, and his need to rid himself of her was because he could not afford to support his wife, their children, and the other bride that he sought after. Soraya's story was recounted by her aunt, to a French journalist, and it provides an example of how barbaric these acts of violence against women are, while also illustrating how vulnerable women are in various societies and within their families. This vulnerability stems from the fact that a family's honor is tied to a girl's/woman's body, ultimately stripping them of their rights to decide how to adorn their body, in which settings to allow themselves to take up space, whose company they can keep, and most importantly who they share their bodies with. There was also the movie *Sound of Tears*, made by Cameroonian director Dorothy Atabong and set in Canada. The movie followed the lead protagonist, a young woman and immigrant, who made the decision to forego a pre-arranged marriage in order to run-off with the man who she loved, and whose child she carried; a man who happened to be White. The movie ends with her being murdered by her brother, and closes with a scene of her mother knowingly sitting in a chair, waiting to receive confirmation that the deed had been done.

These twisted and illogical beliefs allow people within these communities to deem the act of murder as "honorable," or capable of restoring honor, and these outdated beliefs continue to be a problem in the modern world, where according to United Nations statistics, some 5,000 "honor" killings are reported a year, worldwide. This count, of course, does not include the murders that go unreported. Further, they are not a problem that only affects those living in the Middle East or Africa, as there have been cases taking place in the United States, Europe, and Canada. In 2015, a report found that there were 23 to 27 documented honor killings in the United States each year (again, does not capture what is undocumented). In 2009, a report released by the Council of Europe warned that so-called honor killings were far more extensive in Europe than previously believed. The Department of Justice of Canada has even launched a preliminary examination of so-called honor killings.

These acts of violence carried out against women by their relatives should not be referred to as "honor killings" because they are actually dishonorable in nature. There simply is no honor in carrying out brutal and premeditated murder. Therefore, I offer a few suggestions to replace the term "honor killings":

- Family-Directed Killings
- Patriarchal Killings

Masculinity So Fragile

What these acts of violence against women and girls, and in some cases men, particularly LGBTQ men, make clear is that masculinity is extremely fragile, in that the actions of another, and what they choose to say or do with their bodies, allows men to feel as if their masculinity has been diminished and their honor ruined. Any time someone chooses to tie their worth and dignity to the actions of another, it speaks to their fragility. It also speaks to their need to overcompensate and protect their fragile masculinity through the use of brute force and oppression.

Ultimately, masculinity is so fragile and readily becomes problematic because it is often steeped in patriarchy, which not only oppresses and negatively impacts women and girls, but also the men who have to uphold it. Patriarchy dictates to them what actions are deemed acceptable, such as what color clothes they should wear, how close they can respectfully sit next to another man, as well as making it shameful to cry or show any emotion. Consequently, patriarchy makes masculinity fragile, leaving men in a constant and daily battle to protect it. This constant assertion of manhood is often done at the expense of women and girls, and is carried out through oppressive and sexist cultural and social norms, and in some cases through public policy. An example of the political aspect would be laws such as those in Saudi Arabia which prohibit women from driving. To be clear, it is not an official or state law, but one that is upheld by societal views, based on deeply held religious beliefs of clerics who wield a great deal of power and influence. They argue that female drivers "undermine social values." There has been a great deal of pushback to these archaic beliefs, such as the 2011 campaign "Women2Drive" organized by women in Saudi Arabia, which encourage women to disregard the laws and to even dare to post images of themselves driving on social media in an attempt to raise awareness and spark dialogue for reform. Unfortunately, campaigns such as this have not been a major success, and women continue to face punishment for getting behind the wheel of a vehicle. In this case, masculinity is so fragile that the mere thought of women being able to move about freely without the approval and assistance of men is viewed as a challenge to their manhood—a manhood that once again depends on the actions of another.

So, this is what makes masculinity so fragile—the fact that it can be diminished and stripped away by the actions of another. It is extremely problematic in that the ways in which men must prove their masculinity—through specific labels and behaviors —often result in mental, emotional, and physical consequences for both men and women.

Your Honor Cannot Be Based on Ownership of Women's and Girl's Bodies

The most critical problem with "honor" killings is the fact that the entire concept of honor is based on ownership of women's bodies. The ability to dictate what the women in one's family does with their bodies, and being able to show or prove that they have adhered to these rules, and have not rebelled or done what is forbidden. Even when the forbidden involves them taking agency over their bodies and lives.

This cannot be stated in a more simple manner—No one's honor can be based on the ownership of women's and girl's bodies.

A joke made by comedian Chris Rock comes to mind when thinking about this topic of honor-by-ownership. It is a joke where he shared that his "Only job in life is to ensure that his daughters stay off of a pole," or something to that effect. Basically, stating that his honor as a man and success as a father is inherently tied to his daughters' sexuality and personal decisions. One can only imagine what would occur if father's of the millions who engage in sex work, such as strippers, decided that their daughter's profession was so dishonorable that they too had to be punished by death. Another problem with the joke is that it exemplifies the sexist views held by many, and reinforced by both women and men. It is the same view that deeply condemns, vilifies, and looks down upon the strippers but not the men who spend their money and time to simply gaze at naked women's bodies. Their morality is not called to the table. Also, these views are the same that criminalize prostitutes while not applying the same degree of scrutiny and punishment to the johns that pay for sexual services. In many societies, including those in the Western World that likes to pretend it is more progressive, prostitutes – including those who are forced into sex trafficking— are ostracized, while the men who exploit prostitutes are again often free from shame and public scrutiny. Many former prostitutes or those still engaged in this work often speak about this shame and how it affects their ability to return home to their communities, villages, etc. and ever have a "normal life."

These "honor" killings uphold a patriarchal dichotomy that views women as either *Virtuous* or *Whores*. There is no in-between, and worse yet men are not held to similar standards. They are not deemed to be whores based on the number of sexual partners that they may have had, or their chosen style of dress. In fact, the opposite occurs. Men are praised for their sexual prowess, and are often referred to as "lady's men" when their sexual exploits gain notoriety. Even within cultures where these "honor" killings take place, men are not condemned to death or shunned if they engage in premarital sex, sex with prostitutes, or sex outside of their marriages. These acts are acceptable because of the perceived belief that men have sexual needs and desires that must be fulfilled, while ignoring the fact that women may have the same. So, men can engage in dishonorable and immoral activities as long as they have control over women's bodies. This control can be used to ensure that their honor remains intact.

Before We Condemn, Let's Discuss Western Hypocrisy

When hearing about these so-called honor killings it is easy to respond with condemnation, as well as xenophobic reactions about a certain culture and religion—particularly Islam—but the truth of the matter is that those responses are hypocritical. Violence against women, particularly rape culture, is just as problematic for women in the West, and within other cultures and societies. Sure, those carrying out these acts may not be carried out primarily by relatives (although incest, pedophilia, intimate partner violence is often carried out by relatives), it does not take away from the fact that women and girls are victimized by gender-based sexual violence. A recent study in the UK, referred to as the "*Femicide Census,*" found that the vast majority of homicides and violence committed against women were due to the result of intimate partner violence. These killings may not be motivated by a need to restore "honor," but they have commonality in the need to control women and their bodies. If the United States government would restore funding for gun violence research originally earmarked by the 1996 Dickey Amendment (which interestingly restricted the CDC from using its funding to "advocate or promote gun control"), I am quite sure that a similar pattern regarding homicide and women would be revealed. One-hundred and forty-one medical, public health, and social organizations, including the Southern California Public Health Association, for which I serve as President, have joined in on a coalition being led by Doctors for America, which is urging Congress to Restore Funding for Gun Violence Research. Letters have been sent directly to four senior members of the House and Senate Appropriations Committee.

The language used to discuss violence against women and girls is quite problematic globally, because it is steeped in patriarchy and masculine fragility which normalize victim blaming. Those who speak out against street harassment and molestation are simply told that they are being whiny and cannot take a compliment, even when that compliment involves another person believing that they have a right to place their hands on another's body. These arguments are being made despite the fact that women/girls have been killed for simply stating "no"—for saying that they did not want to give a man their number or didn't want to stay in a relationship with a man. One of the most graphic examples of this occurred when a young woman was stabbed to death in the middle of a crowded commuter train in Chicago. At the root of these retaliatory acts of violence is the fact that these men felt not only rejected, but as if they had been dissed—and thus disrespected. In other words, they too believed that their honor was diminished.

Normalized language of violence against women/girls made it possible for people like Daniel Holtzclaw, a former Oklahoma police officer convicted in December 2015 of rape, sexual battery, forcible sodomy and other charges, to sexually abuse and exploit women; as well as for the exploitation of Celeste Guap in Oakland, California, who has spoken out about engaging in sexual acts (while under the age of legal consent) with dozens of police officers from throughout the Bay Area under the guise of protection. Guap's ordeal has led to a scandal that involves the resignation of a number of police chiefs. In each case, the women involved remained silent because of the way they are viewed in society, and referred to by the media. They are rarely seen as the victim, and in other cases victims are simply blamed for what has transpired against them. This is the basis of rape culture, and rape culture has become so toxic with the advent of social media that men have used these platforms to harass, stalk, and make threats of rape and murder against women.

In consummation, the current language used to describe violence against women and girls is beyond problematic. It helps to perpetuate patriarchal views of ownership and control of women and their bodies, particularly in the use of the term "honor killings," which ties a man's perceived honor to the choices made by a woman, regarding her life and body. There is absolutely no "honor" in killing.

References

Matthew A. Goldstein, "The biological roots of heat-of-passion crimes and honour killings," *Politics and the Life Sciences* 21,2 (2002): 28-37.

William Blackstone, *Commentaries on the Laws of England*, 1765-1769, *Book Four, Public Wrongs*, (Oxford, Clarendon Press, 1769, reprinted by Wildy & Sons Ltd., London, 1966): 181.

James A. Brundage, *Law, Sex and Christian Society in Medieval Europe*, Chicago: University of Chicago Press, 1987, 55.

Support Victims of Violence Around the World

UN Women

In the following viewpoint, The United Nations Entity for Gender Equality and the Empowerment of Women demands that certain fundamental provisions be included in laws aimed at assisting women targeted by honor-based violence. In addition, UN Women argues for the repeal of laws that detain or relocate victims and seeks to vigorously prosecute those that perpetuate the violence. The United Nations Entity for Gender Equality and the Empowerment of Women, established under the UN General Assembly, champions women's issues.

As you read, consider the following questions:

1. Immediate family members of victims might play what opposing roles?
2. Which two countries are cited as having promising practices?
3. What is the effective ratio of crisis center to population?

Protection, Support and Assistance for Victims

Victims may include the direct target of the harmful practice, as well as her immediate family. However, when drafting provisions on the rights of victims of harmful practices, drafters should take

UN Women (2012) Victim services: Protection support and Assistance for victims, Web article from the Virtual Knowledge Centre to End Violence against Women and Girls: endvawnow.org.

into account that her immediate family may be the perpetrators or accomplices to the crime. Laws should clearly delineate that, for purposes of this section, victims do not include any person who perpetrated, authorized, aided, abetted or otherwise solicited the harmful practice, regardless of their relationship to the victim.

- Drafters should ensure that laws include provision for funding for comprehensive and integrated support services to assist victims of harmful practices crimes.

- For example, with regards to honour crimes, the Council of Europe Parliamentary Assembly Resolution 1681 (2009) recommends that states provide shelter that is geographically accessible to victims, develop long-term physical and psychological support programs for victims, facilitate economic independence of victims, and provide police protection and a new identify, if needed.

- Drafters should provide for a free, 24-hour hotline that is accessible from anywhere in the country, offers assistance in multiple languages, and is staffed by persons trained in issues related to harmful practice.

- Drafters should provide sufficient shelters for victims of harmful practices located in both rural and urban areas, which can accommodate victims and their children for emergency stays and which will help them to find a refuge for longer stays. The decision to stay at a shelter should always be made voluntarily by the victim. Drafters ensure that special accommodation is made for girls under 18 years of age who are at risk for harmful practices. Shelter policies and accommodations should take into account the special needs of immigrant women and girls.

- Legislation should provide adequate resources for shelters to provide resources and support to victims of harmful practices. If shelters for domestic violence are used to receive victims of harmful practices, shelter workers and advocates should be adequately trained to address issues specific and unique to various harmful practices.

- Drafters should repeal any laws or orders that allow the practice of detaining women who are victims of harmful practices. The focus should be on arresting the perpetrators rather than detaining or relocating the victims. Drafters should adopt laws ordering the immediate release of victims of harmful practices who have been detained without charge, process or review; repeal laws that precondition a woman's release on the custody of a male relative or husband; and, upon release, ensure victims' full protection and facilitate voluntary placement in a shelter for women victims of violence, if the victim so desires.

Where shelters are lacking, some governments have incarcerated victims in prisons to protect them from honour crimes. This practice should be avoided. For example, in Jordan, no shelters exist for victims of honour crimes, and state authorities often place these women in involuntary detention in the Jweideh Correctional and Rehabilitation Center. An administrative governor may detain without due process any person in protective custody to ensure public safety, a practice regularly applied to females who are at risk of being subjected to honour-based violence. Once detained under the governor's order, only his consent will secure her release, which is generally granted only when he believes she can leave safely and a male relative agrees to assume responsibility for her.

- Drafters should provide one crisis center for every 50,000 population, with trained staff to provide support, legal advice, and crisis intervention counseling for victims of harmful practices, including specialized services for particular groups such as immigrants.

- Crisis centers should be prepared and adequately trained to deal with victims before, during and after the harmful practice.

- Accreditation standards for the assistance centers described above should be developed in consultation with NGOs and advocates working directly with complainants/ survivors.

- Drafters should provide for access to health care for immediate injuries and long-term care including reproductive health care and HIV prophylaxis.

- Health care should be adequately resourced to address the particular injuries, such as burns or disfiguration that victims of harmful practices may have sustained. Victims of FGM should receive services for their immediate injuries but also for the long-term consequences of the practice.

- As with domestic violence, a coordinated community response is an essential component of the response to harmful practices.

- Drafters should provide for aid, including shelter, clothing and food, for the children of a victim of harmful practices in the shelters described above.

- A state agency should be assigned to establish the aid centers described above, by providing general guidelines or standards, and the state agency should be mandated to fund all of the above services.

Promising Practice: United Kingdom— UK's Women's National Commission

The UK's Women's National Commission is a national body that liaises between the women's rights advocates and government to promote women's equality. The commission is state-funded yet free to comment on government policy. The Women's National Commission established a Violence Against Women Working Group, with two sub-groups on sexual violence and domestic violence, which seeks:

1. To promote understanding and awareness of violence against women and effect changes in laws, policy and practice;

2. To monitor implementation of Government Action Plans;

3. To co-ordinate Women's National Commission member views on violence against women and to ensure that these views are represented to policy-makers;

4. To liaise with other Women's National Commission Groups on relevant aspects of work;

5. To produce reports in response to national and international developments; and

6. To liaise with Government departments, other non-departmental public bodies, and relevant NGO policy working groups.

Protesters in Jordan Seek to Dismantle Sexist Legislation

Nora B for Global Voices

In this article, the author reports on an organized protest against Jordanian laws that allow perpetrators of honor killings to walk free. Nora B—a Saudi Arabian researcher based in Amman, Jordan—breaks down the country's misogynistic penal code, talks to protesters, and discusses what can be done to end the cycle of honor-based violence.

As you read, consider the following questions:

1. What are the ramifications of Article 98 of the Jordanian Penal Code?
2. What does the organization I Change hope to accomplish?
3. How do attitudes of ninth graders in Jordan differ from those of high school students in the U.S.?

O n February 1, 2017, a group of around 25-30 protesters peacefully gathered in front of the Jordanian parliament in Amman's Abdali district to call for the repeal of Article 340 of the Jordanian Penal Code, which allows for perpetrators of "honour killing" to benefit from mitigation. Global Voices' Nora B attended the protest.

So-called honour killings are acts of deadly vengeance

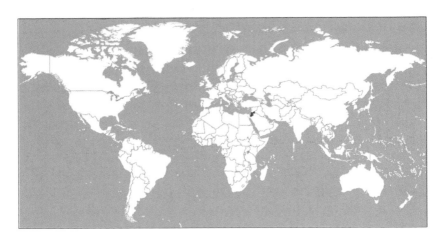

committed by male family members against female family members who are perceived to have tainted the family name. In 2016, there were 26 cases of honour killings in Jordan, nine more than in 2015. Reasons for such murders could be premarital sex or as arbitrary as having a secret phone that the family does not know about.

Articles 340 and 98 of the Penal Code allow for reduced sentences for honour killings, with the text of the former stating that whoever finds his wife or one of his female relatives in an act of adultery benefits from mitigation if he murders her and/ or her partner.

Article 98 also allows perpetrators of honour killings to have a less severe sentence, with its text stating, "Whoever commits a crime while in a state of rage which is the result of an unjustifiable and dangerous act committed by the victim, benefits from a mitigating excuse." Sentences could be as light as six months or less if the victim's family decides to drop the charges, as seen in the case of a pregnant woman suffocated to death in 2007 by her own brother after confessing to him that she was five months pregnant with her ex-husband's child, or the case of a brother murdering his divorced sister in 2003 for being absent from the family home for one week.

There have been previous attempts to repeal the article in parliament, but none succeeded; instead, it was amended in

2001 to give the right of a mitigated sentence to women as well. However, the amendment only applies in cases of assault or murder of husbands, and does not extend to women's brothers or family members, whereas the article states that men can benefit from mitigation if they murder their wives or female relatives. To date, reported honour killing victims in Jordan have always been women.

The protest was organised by 17-year-old Esraa Tayseer Kudair on behalf of a group called "I Change." Esraa is a high-school student passionate about advancing women's status in the country, starting with the repeal of the Article 340. "There are women that are being killed without doing anything wrong, and people are using this law to justify the killing these women," she told Global Voices.

Some of the slogans on posters in the protest read: "Article 340 allows for murder and encourages it," "Kill her, you will be protected," "Justifying crime is a crime," "There is no honour in killing," and "Reform begins with repealing Article 340 from the Jordanian Penal Code."

Feras Awad, a master's student of Women's Studies at the University of Jordan who was present at the protest, addressed the members of parliament as they were exiting the parliamentary building: "This article represents a license to kill, and allows for the murder of women just because they are women," he said through a loudspeaker. "Times and circumstances have changed: it wasn't suitable then, and it isn't suitable now."

Two members of parliament, Nawaf al-Nuaimat and Suleiman Huwailah al-Zabn, approached the activists at different points. Al-Zabn addressed the crowd and answered questions, saying "We must hold killers accountable, we are with you. I am with you as a member of parliament, as are my peers. We are working towards this direction." The members of parliament gave their contact details to the organisers of the protest and encouraged them to get in touch and follow up, with al-Nuaimat suggesting that two representatives from the group attend a future session.

Fighting the law is one thing, but cultural attitudes towards honour killings are worrying still. In 2013, a survey of around 850 ninth grade students in the capital Amman revealed that about 40% of boys and 20% of girls believe that honour killings can be justified. "I Change" is trying to change these attitudes as well as the laws. "I Change is a group of people that are gathered for a reason: to protect women from honour crimes and to educate people on this matter," Esraa told Global Voices. She says that if this campaign succeeds, I Change might work on other reform projects in the kingdom.

Changing Societal Norms Worldwide Could Save Lives

World Health Organization

The following publication from the World Health Organization (WHO) claims that rules or expected behavior within groups, both cultural or social, can encourage violence. WHO reports that strategies to prevent violent acts require interventions that challenge and ultimately change attitudes of the population within targeted groups. Deeply held beliefs—and the resulting honor killings—may take a very long time to change.

As you read, consider the following questions:

1. What causes social acceptance of violent behavior?
2. What behaviors were changed by mass media campaigns?
3. Which group of people plays a large part in preventing sexual abuse in the United States?

Overview

Cultural and social norms can encourage violence

Rules or expectations of behaviour—norms—within a cultural or social group can encourage violence. Interventions that challenge cultural and social norms supportive of violence can prevent acts of violence and have been widely used. This briefing describes how cultural and social norms can support violence, gives examples of interventions that aim to alter such norms and identifies the main challenges to rigorously evaluating such interventions.

Interventions often target intimate partner and youth violence.

Some aim to reduce dating violence and sexual abuse among teenagers and young adults by challenging attitudes and norms related to gender that, for instance, allow men control over women. Many work with male peer groups, acknowledging the strong influence that young adults can have on each others' behaviour. A common approach aims to correct misperceptions that people may have of the attitudes and behaviour of others. Mass media campaigns, including education through entertainment (*edutainment*), have also been used to challenge norms supportive of violence.

Laws and policies can assist in altering norms linked to violence.

Laws and policies that make violent behaviour an offence send a message to society that it is not acceptable. While nearly all governments around the world have laws against most forms of homicide, recently more governments have begun to enact and implement laws against non-lethal intimate partner violence.

Introduction

Cultural and social norms are highly influential in shaping individual behaviour, including the use of violence. Norms can protect against violence, but they can also support and encourage the use of it. For instance, cultural acceptance of violence, either as a normal method of resolving conflict or as a usual part of rearing a child, is a risk factor for all types of interpersonal violence. It may also help explain why countries experiencing high levels of one type of violence also experience increased levels of other types. Social tolerance of violent behaviour is likely learned in childhood, through the use of corporal punishment or witnessing violence in the family, in the media or in other settings.

Interventions that challenge cultural and social norms supportive of violence can help reduce and prevent violent behaviour. Although widely used, they have rarely been evaluated. Given the current weak evidence base, it is premature to review their effectiveness. The aim of this briefing, therefore, is to encourage increased efforts to implement and evaluate well-designed interventions that challenge cultural and social norms which support violence. Accordingly, this briefing:

- Defines cultural and social norms and illustrates how they support violence;

- Provides examples of interventions that seek to alter these norms; and

- Identifies the main challenges faced by evaluations of the effectiveness of such interventions.

Cultural and Social Norms That Support Violence

Cultural and social norms are rules or expectations of behaviour within a specific cultural or social group. Often unspoken, these norms offer social standards of appropriate and inappropriate behaviour, governing what is (and is not) acceptable and coordinating our interactions with others. Cultural and social norms persist within society because of individuals' preference to conform, given the expectation that others will also conform. A variety of external and internal pressures are thought to maintain cultural and social norms. Thus, individuals are discouraged from violating norms by the threat of social disapproval or punishment and feelings of guilt and shame that result from the internalization of norms.

Cultural and social norms do not necessarily correspond with an individual's attitudes (positive or negative feelings towards an object or idea) and beliefs (perceptions that certain premises are true), although they may influence these attitudes and beliefs if norms becomes internalized. Cultural and social norms also vary widely; so, behaviour acceptable to one social group, gang or culture may not be tolerated in another.

Different cultural and social norms support different types of violence .For instance, traditional beliefs that men have a right to control or discipline women through physical means makes women vulnerable to violence by intimate partners and places girls at risk of sexual abuse. Equally, cultural acceptance of violence, including sexual violence, as a private affair hinders outside intervention and prevents those affected from speaking out and gaining support. In many societies, victims of sexual violence also feel stigmatized, which inhibits reporting.

Additionally, strong evidence of an association between alcohol consumption and violent behaviour means that cultural and social norms around alcohol use and its expected effects can also encourage and justify violent acts. In a number of countries, harmful alcohol use is estimated to be responsible for 26% of male and 16% of female disability-adjusted life-years (DALYs) lost as a result of homicide. Societies that tolerate higher rates of acute alcohol intoxication report stronger relationships between alcohol use and violence than those where drinking occurs more moderately. Furthermore, alcohol-related violence is considered more likely in cultures where many believe that alcohol plays a positive role by helping people to shed their inhibitions. Here, alcohol can be used as a justification for violent behaviour, or consumed to fuel the courage needed to commit violent crimes. Interventions that tackle the cultural and social norms underlying risky drinking behaviour and social expectations surrounding alcohol can help in preventing violence. For more information on the relationship between alcohol and violence, see the briefing in this series on preventing violence by reducing the availability and harmful use of alcohol.

Cultural and Social Norms Supporting Different Types of Violence

Child maltreatment

- Female children are valued less in society than males (e.g. Peru, where female children are considered to have less social and economic potential).

- Children have a low status in society and within the family (e.g. Guatemala).

- Physical punishment is an acceptable or normal part of rearing a child (e.g. Turkey, Ethiopia).

- Communities adhere to harmful traditional cultural practices such as genital mutilation (e.g. Nigeria, Sudan) or child marriage.

Intimate partner violence

- A man has a right to assert power over a woman and is socially superior (e.g. India, Nigeria, Ghana).

- A man has a right to "correct" or discipline female behaviour (e.g. India, Nigeria, China).

- A woman's freedom should be restricted (e.g. Pakistan).

- Physical violence is an acceptable way to resolve conflicts within a relationship (e.g. South Africa, China).

- A woman is responsible for making a marriage work (e.g. Israel).

- Intimate partner violence is a taboo subject (e.g. South Africa) and reporting abuse is disrespectful (Nigeria).

- Divorce is shameful (e.g. Pakistan).

- When a dowry (financial payment from the bride's family to the husband) or bridewealth (financial payment from the husband to the bride's family) is an expected part of marriage (e.g. Nigeria, India), violence can occur either because financial demands are not met, or because bridewealth becomes synonymous with purchasing and thus owning a wife.

- A man's honour is linked to a woman's sexual behaviour. Here, any deviation from sexual norms disgraces the entire family, which can then lead to honour killings (e.g. Jordan).

Suicide and self-harm

- Mental health problems are embarrassing and shameful, deterring individuals from seeking help (e.g. Australia, Brazil).
- Individuals in different social groups within society are not tolerated—e.g. homosexuals (Japan).

Sexual violence

- Sex is a man's right in marriage (e.g. Pakistan).
- Girls are responsible for controlling a man's sexual urges (e.g. South Africa).
- Sexual violence is an acceptable way of putting women in their place or punishing them (e.g. South Africa).
- Sexual activity (including rape) is a marker of masculinity (e.g. South Africa).
- Sex and sexuality are taboo subjects (e.g. Pakistan).
- Sexual violence such as rape is shameful for the victim, which prevents disclosure (e.g. the United States).

Youth violence

- Reporting youth violence or bullying is unacceptable (e.g. the United Kingdom).

- Violence is an acceptable way of resolving conflict (e.g. the United States of America).

Community violence

- Cultural intolerance, intense dislike and stereotyping of "different" groups within society (e.g. nationalities, ethnicities, homosexuals) can contribute to violent or aggressive behaviour towards them (e.g. xenophobic or racist violence and homophobic violence).

Challenging Norms Supportive of Violence: Examples of Interventions

Interventions that challenge cultural and social norms supportive of violence are often integrated with other approaches. The examples described here, however, are limited to those interventions which exclusively or primarily aim to change cultural and social norms to prevent violence. Although not all of them have been evaluated, these examples are presented to help gain a better understanding of this approach to violence prevention. [The section below] sets out the concepts behind the social norms approach, one of the more prominent frameworks for such interventions. A particular challenge for any intervention addressing cultural or social norms is accommodating groups with different norms from the broader population. Interventions often need to be tailored to these sub-groups, rather than addressing the population as a whole.

Social norms approach

The social norms approach to health promotion assumes that people have mistaken perceptions of the attitudes and behaviour of others. Prevalence of risky behaviour (e.g. heavy alcohol use and tolerance of violent behaviour) is usually overestimated, while protective behaviours are normally underestimated. This affects individual behaviour in two ways: by justifying and increasing the prevalence of risky behaviour, and by increasing the likelihood of an individual remaining silent about any discomfort caused by such behaviour (thereby reinforcing social tolerance of it). The social norms approach seeks to correct these misperceptions by giving people a more realistic sense of actual behavioural norms, thereby reducing risky behaviour. The theory has been applied widely in the United States to reduce excessive drinking among college students and has been associated with decreased alcohol misuse and smoking. Social norms approaches have also reported some success in changing the attitudes of male peer groups towards risky sexual behaviours (see section on intimate partner and sexual violence). Misperceptions about attitudes towards violent behaviour have also been documented for bullying, suggesting that social norms approaches could reduce this form of violence.

Intimate partner and sexual violence

In the United States and other developed countries, initiatives have been developed to reduce dating violence and sexual abuse among teenagers and young adults that incorporate components to change cultural and social norms. These norms include gender stereotypes, beliefs about masculinity and aggression or violence and ideas that violence within an intimate or dating relationship is normal. Some initiatives deal specifically with male peer groups, for example, Men of Strength clubs; others target both men and women, for example, Men Against Violence and Mentors in Violence Prevention. Such programmes acknowledge the strong influence that young adults can have on each others' behaviour and the social pressures of masculinity that equate male power and status with violence. By raising awareness of dating violence and reinforcing shared norms supportive of non-violent behaviour, they encourage the role of young adults as allies or protectors of their peers against dating and sexual violence. Furthermore, it is assumed that by challenging and intervening in violent acts, young people will indicate to their peers that such behaviour is unacceptable. Unfortunately, the effectiveness of these programmes for preventing violent behaviour has yet to be well evaluated.

The social norms approach…has been used to address sexual violence among college students in the United States. Among these students, men are thought to underestimate the importance that most men and women place on sexual consent, and the willingness of most men to intervene against sexual assault. Although evidence is limited, some positive results have been reported. For instance, in one university, a project named A Man Respects a Woman aimed to reduce sexual assaults against women, increase accurate perceptions of non-coercive sexual behaviour norms and reduce self-reported coercive behaviours by men. The project used a social norms marketing campaign targeting men, a theatre presentation addressing socialization and male peer- to-peer education to convey the following positive findings of a student survey:

- A man respects a woman:nine out of ten men stop the first time their date says "no" to sexual activity;

- A man always prevents manipulation: three out of four men think it is not acceptable to pressure a date to drink alcohol to improve their chances of getting their date to have sex;

- A man talks before romance: most men believe talking about sex does not ruin the romance of the moment, and it can confirm that you have consent.

For the social marketing campaign, posters and flyers were designed by and pre-tested with students at the university, to ensure the messages would receive positive responses. Evaluation of the campaign two years after implementation found that men had become more accurate in their perceptions of other men's behaviour and reported more positive behaviour and attitudes themselves. For instance, proportionately fewer men believed that the average male student has sex when his partner is intoxicated; will not stop sexual activity when asked to if he is already sexually aroused; and, when wanting to touch someone sexually, tries and sees how his date reacts. The evaluation found, however, an increase in the proportion of men indicating they have sex when their partner is intoxicated.

University campaigns in the United States have also highlighted the role of bystanders in preventing sexually abusive acts—an alternative to targeting perpetrators or victims of violence. These campaigns address norms that support or tolerate coercion within relationships and encourage both males and females to speak out against sexual abuse and to help those in trouble. For instance, a poster campaign at one university used this message: "Know your power. Step in, speak up. You can make a difference". A series of posters was widely displayed for four weeks on campus and nearby, depicting different scenarios: for instance, a man leading a drunk woman upstairs at a house party. Each poster also showed safe bystander behaviour to intervene and prevent sexual abuse: for instance, friends planning to stop the man from taking the woman upstairs. Although there was no baseline test for comparison, an evaluation of the campaign reported that participants who saw the posters exhibited greater awareness of sexual assault, and greater willingness to participate in actions aimed at reducing sexual violence, compared to those who did not see the posters.

In Western Australia, the Freedom from Fear campaign targeted male perpetrators (and potential perpetrators) of domestic violence. Preliminary research with male perpetrators found that campaign messages such as "real men don't hit women" and "your mates will reject you," or those highlighting the consequences of domestic violence on their partner, would be ineffective. However, those that conveyed the damaging effect that intimate partner violence had on their children were found to be powerful, and were consequently given prominence in the campaign. The messages called upon men to accept responsibility for their behaviour and take action to end the abuse. It used television, radio and other media, and was accompanied by a helpline for men to receive counselling, advice and information. Evaluation of the campaign five years after implementation found a smaller proportion of men reporting emotional abuse of their partners than before the campaign. Furthermore, there was a significant reduction in the proportion of women who reported "being yelled at" and "being threatened with being hit."

Another promising campaign, Choose Respect, is a national initiative developed by the United States Centers for Disease Control and Prevention to address cultural and social norms governing relationships and partner violence. It aims to motivate adolescents to challenge harmful beliefs about dating abuse and take steps to form healthy, respectful relationships and prevent dating abuse before it starts. Research to inform the initiative showed most adolescents have positive, healthy attitudes about their relationships with others. Choose Respect seeks to reinforce and sustain these positive attitudes among adolescents as they get older and begin to enter dating relationships by:

- Encouraging adolescents, parents, caregivers and teachers to choose to treat themselves and others with respect;

- Creating opportunities for adolescents and parents to learn positive forms of behaviour for relationships;

- Increasing adolescents' ability to recognize and prevent unhealthy, violent relationships; and

- Promoting ways for a variety of audiences to get information and other tools to prevent dating abuse.

Choose Respect targets 11 to 14-years-olds, an age group whose members are still forming attitudes and beliefs that will affect how they are treated and treat others. The initiative also engages parents, teachers, youth leaders and other caregivers who influence the lives of young teens. Its messages are disseminated via materials such as electronic postcards (eCards), posters, bookmarks, pocket guides, online games and quizzes, television and radio spots and activities that encourage youth to choose respect. Launched nationally in May 2006, Choose Respect was implemented as an integrated communications effort in ten major cities in the United States.

To highlight social issues, including intimate partner violence, date rape and sexual harassment, Soul City in South Africa used television (through a soap opera series), radio and printed materials (i.e. edutainment). The series was accompanied by information booklets that were distributed nationally. An evaluation of the fourth series, which focused on intimate partner violence, used a random sample of the national population and conducted interviews before and after the intervention (eight month interval). Participants reported a decrease in their acceptance of intimate partner violence and an increase in the belief that communities can play a role in preventing intimate partner violence following the series. For instance, there was an increase from baseline to evaluation eight months later in the belief that "my community feels that violence between a man and a woman is not a private affair." The intervention was thought to facilitate community cooperation, public discussion and action on intimate partner violence. While the evaluation did not include measurements of violent behaviour, there were some positive changes in attitudes towards intimate partner violence. For instance, the number of people *agreeing* with the statement "no woman ever deserves to be beaten" increased, as did the percentage *disagreeing* with the assertion "women who are abused are expected to put up with it." While it is not known whether these changes would have occurred without the intervention (there was no comparison group), higher exposure to the intervention was associated with more positive attitudinal changes.

Another programme that used *edutainment* is Nicaragua's *Somos Diferentes, Somos Iguales* (We are Different, We are Equal), which aimed primarily to prevent HIV infection. The programme also addressed related topics such as gender-based violence, aiming to empower women and young people and to promote women's rights and gender equality. It used a national weekly soap opera television series (*Sexto Sentido* [Sixth Sense]); a nightly radio talk show, in which callers could discuss the issues raised by the television series; and community-based activities such as youth leadership training. An evaluation of the project used a sample of 13 to 24-year-old Nicaraguan youths and surveyed them over a period of two years. Although there was no comparison group, exposure to the programme was associated with greater acceptance of gender equality as a social norm. The study did not measure changes in violent behaviour.

Mass media interventions

Mass media campaigns convey messages about healthy behaviour to broad populations via television, radio, the Internet, newspapers, magazines and other printed materials. They increase the amount of information available on a topic and may reduce undesirable behaviour. Media campaigns use different strategies to change cultural and social norms. For instance, they can provide information to correct misperceptions about norms (social norms approach), or attach a social stigma to unwanted behaviour. While campaigns usually focus on the negative consequences of violence, they may also make positive appeals—for example, promoting parenting styles that contribute to a happier family life.

Mass media approaches help to keep health issues on social and political agendas, legitimize community interventions and act as a catalyst for other initiatives (60). While they intend to modify individual behaviour directly through informative messages, media campaigns can also affect behaviour indirectly by stimulating changes in perceptions of social or cultural norms through social interaction. Here, a change in perception of norms provides additional motivation for a change in individual behaviour. Some mass media approaches use education entertainment methods (*edutainment*), which seek to impart knowledge and bring about social change through television soap operas and other popular forms of entertainment. By achieving strong audience identification with television characters who are positive role models, edutainment can contribute to help improve cultural and social norms.

Mass media campaigns have been successfully employed to address a wide range of health attitudes and behaviour, such as eating healthily and exercising, stopping smoking, practising safe sex, reducing alcohol consumption and reducing drink-driving. A meta-analysis of 48 health-behaviour campaigns reported that on average, 9% more people exhibited a healthy form of behaviour following a campaign than before. Mass media campaigns have also been used to address violence. Few studies, however, have evaluated their effectiveness at reducing violence. By contrast, many studies have examined the effectiveness of other campaigns to promote healthy behaviour.

Among the factors that seem to contribute to the success of mass media campaigns are messages about legal penalties for non-compliant behaviour, fresh information (i.e. a new recommended behaviour to solve a health problem) and reaching a large proportion of the intended audience. In addition, success is more likely if messages are tailored to audiences using social marketing principles and creating a supportive environment that enables the intended audience to make changes—e.g. by mobilizing communities in support of the campaign. To develop effective campaigns, it is also important to use research, such as interviews with key stakeholders and focus groups with members of the target audience, to determine existing attitudes and beliefs and ways of motivating people to change their behaviour. Campaign messages should also be pre-tested among target audiences to ensure they are understood correctly and to minimize any unintended negative effects on other audiences.

Youth violence

In the United States, an anti-violence intervention called Resolve It, Solve It consisted of a community media campaign for youths from small towns, led by high-school students who served as peer models. Students helped develop campaign media such as professionally printed materials and radio and television advertisements with three key themes: respect for individual differences, conflict resolution and prevention of bullying. The campaign ran for a year and included presentations to school children in classrooms and assemblies, and inclusion of a wider audience via community events. A randomized controlled trial of the campaign conducted in communities in five different states showed mixed results. A few months after the intervention, students reported a greater decline in their use of physical violence compared to controls, but there were no differences in their use of verbal aggression. Additionally, compared to controls, participants reported a larger decline in being verbally, but not physically victimized. However, effects differed by sex.

Laws and policies

Legislation can be a key tool in changing behaviour and perceptions of cultural and social norms. Laws and policies that make violent behaviour an offence send a message to society that it is not acceptable. Countries differ in the laws applied to violent behaviour. While nearly all countries have laws that criminalize most forms of homicide, only some countries have laws in place to protect women from intimate partner violence, or children from caregiver maltreatment. However, there has been a recent move internationally towards the enactment and implementation of such laws; particularly for intimate partner violence where there has been increased international activity to promote women's rights. For example, laws on domestic violence have recently been implemented in Brazil (2006), Ghana (2007), India (2006) and Zimbabwe (2006). Confounding factors make it difficult to evaluate the effects of laws and policies on cultural and social norms and violent behaviour. Furthermore, the introduction of legislation that makes violent behaviour a criminal offence increases rates of reported violence, making trends from official statistics difficult to interpret. Finally, although the implementation of laws may have an effect on behaviour through fear of punishment, changes in deeply held beliefs that justify such behaviour may take far longer to occur.

Summary

Violent behaviour is strongly influenced by cultural and social norms; so efforts to prevent violence must consider how social pressures and expectations influence individual behaviour.

Interventions that attempt to alter cultural and social norms to prevent violence are among the most widespread and prominent. Rarely, however, are they thoroughly evaluated, making it currently difficult to assess their effectiveness. Rigorous scientific evaluations of interventions that address norms supportive of violence present particular, but surmountable, challenges, which partly explain their scarcity. Nevertheless, a number of positive results have been reported.

Although the effect of mass media interventions, aimed at whole societies, on levels of violent behaviour have seldom been evaluated, their success in addressing other public health issues (smoking and drink-driving, for instance) suggests they have a critical role to play in the prevention of violence. Furthermore, *edutainment* initiatives, such as Soul City in South Africa, have shown promise in changing cultural and social norms and attitudes associated with violent behaviour. While it is difficult to ascertain the effectiveness of laws and policies in changing social attitudes, legislation that is enforced can send clear messages to society that violent behaviour is not acceptable.

Periodical and Internet Sources Bibliography

The following articles have been selected to supplement the diverse views presented in this chapter.

Ron Csillag. "Canadian imams declare fatwa against 'honor killings,'" *Christian Century,* vol. 129, issue 5, March 7, 2012, pp. 19-19. www.christiancentury.org/article/2012-02/canadian-imams-issue-fatwa-against-honor-killings.

Maja Daniels. "Honor killing is murder in cold blood," *New Statesman,* vol. 141, issue 5099, April 2, 2012, pp. 32-33.

Jonathan Gatehouse. "CANADA HAS BEEN LUCKY," *Maclean's,* vol. 122, issue 31, August 17, 2009, pp. 24-25.

Naila Inayat. "In Pakistan, law closes honor killings loophole," *USA Today,* October 7, 2016. http://www.usatoday.com/story/news/world/2016/10/06/pakistani-law-cracks-down-honor-killing/91677520/.

Rishi Iyengar. "After Social Media Star's Murder, Pakistan Will Move to Outlaw 'Honor Killings,'" *Time.com,* July 21, 2016, pp. 168-168. http://time.com/4416510/pakistan-honor-killing-qandeel-baloch-law-maryam-nawaz-sharif/.

Salman Masood. "Pakistan Toughens Laws on Rape and 'Honor Killings' of Women," *New York Times,* October 6, 2016. https://www.nytimes.com/2016/10/07/world/asia/pakistan-toughens-laws-on-rape-and-honor-killings-of-women.html.

Jo McGowan. "Above the Law, Beneath Contempt," *Commonweal,* vol. 137, issue 15, September 10, 2010, pp. 6.

Alasdair Soussi. "Honour Killings," *Canadian Dimension,* vol. 39, issue 2, March/April, 2005, pp. 16-17.

Theresa Wolfwood. "Amnesty Vows to Dishonour 'Honour' Killings," *Herizons,* vol. 19, issue 1, Summer, 2005, pp. 6-7.

For Further Discussion

Chapter 1

1. According to Phyllis Chesler, honor killing is not a form of Western-style domestic violence. Use one other author's viewpoint to support or disprove Chesler's supposition.
2. Compare the views of at least two authors from chapter one concerning the number of honor killings worldwide and the reasons stated for this violence.

Chapter 2

1. What is the most influential cause of honor killing? Support your view with evidence and facts from two of this chapter's authors.
2. Compare and contrast the views on Islamic law put forth in the viewpoints. What do these authors agree on, and how do their views differ?
3. Is violence against women in non-Islamic countries any different from what's traditionally considered an honor killing?

Chapter 3

1. Provide evidence from two authors demonstrating that incidences of honor killings are on the rise worldwide.
2. Compare and contrast the state of honor killings in the Middle East and Asia to the honor-based crimes occurring in Europe and the United States.

Chapter 4

1. Will renaming honor killing help stem violence against women?
2. How can grassroots activism in countries dealing with honor-based crimes help or harm the issue of honor killings?

Organizations to Contact

The editors have compiled the following list of organizations concerned with the issues debated in this book. The descriptions are derived from materials provided by the organizations. All have publications or information available for interested readers. The list was compiled on the date of publication of the present volume; the information provided here may change. Be aware that many organizations take several weeks or longer to respond to inquiries, so allow as much time as possible.

Amnesty International (AI)
1 Easton Street
London WC1X 0DW
United Kingdom
phone: (44) 20 7413 5500
fax: (44) 20 7956 1157
website: www.amnesty.org

Amnesty International is an organization comprising more than seven million people from all corners of the globe. Without any political, economic, or religious ties, they have joined together to fight for human rights. This group believes that in every situation and every government there is hope for oppressed individuals. For more than fifty years this dedicated team has supported the idea of freedom and dignity for all. AI conducts research, disseminates reports, and four times per year publishes its magazine, *WIRE*, to inspire and inform members and the world at large.

Forced Marriage Unit (FMU)
Foreign and Commonwealth Office and Home Office
King Charles Street
London SW1A 2AH
United Kingdom
phone: 44 (0) 20 7008 0151
email: fmu@fco.gov.uk
website: www.gov.uk/guidance/forced-marriage

The Forced Marriage Unit is a branch of the Foreign and Commonwealth Office in the United Kingdom that provides assistance to victims of forced marriage and to professionals dealing with this issue. The organization operates both in the United Kingdom and overseas, offering a wide range of services—even potential rescue of victims held overseas against their will. The agency produces a variety of educational items and media campaigns and includes a brochure titled, "What Is a Forced Marriage?"

Human Rights Watch (HRW)
350 Fifth Avenue, 34th floor
New York, NY 10118-3299
phone: 1-212-290-4700
fax: 1-212-736-1300
website: www.hrw.org

Human Rights Watch is a nonprofit keeping watch over conditions affecting human rights in about ninety countries worldwide. Through an extensive workforce, this agency provides factual, accurate, and ethical investigation that, in turn, is used to pressure those in power to respect human rights and dignity for all individuals. Besides weekly newsletters and online reporting HRW publishes an annual report.

International Women's Rights Action Watch (IWRAW)

University of Minnesota Human Rights Center
229 19th Avenue South
Minneapolis, MN 55455
phone: 1-612-625-49851
fax: 1-612-625-2011
website: hrlibrary.umn.edu/iwraw/index.html

The International Women's Rights Action Watch was organized at the Third World Conference on Women to seek justice for women's rights via international human rights treaties—including the United Nations Convention on the Elimination of All Forms of Discrimination against Women. Affiliated with the University of Minnesota, the IWRAW manages a resource center that works with researchers throughout the world. Their tools for advocacy include manuals and guides for NGOs such as "Assessing the Status of Women in the 21st Century: A Guide to Monitoring and Reporting on Women's Human Rights under the CEDAW Convention."

Karma Nirvana

PO Box 515
Leeds LS6 9DW
United Kingdom
phone: 0800 5999 247
email: info@karmanirvana.org.uk
website: www.karmanirvana.org.uk

Karma Nirvana is an organization dedicated to saving and improving the lives of victims of honor-based violence and forced marriages. The agency staffs a helpline for both victims of violence and professionals engaging in treatment. This group also educates through their roadshows and campaigns, and trains police with strategies to support crime victims. Karma Nirvana publishes a monthly newsletter to share updates on their work.

National Council of Canadian Muslims (NCCM)

PO Box 13219
Ottawa, ON K2K 1X4
Canada
phone: 1-866-524-0004
fax: 613-254-9810
website: www.nccm.ca

The National Council of Canadian Muslims is an independent, nonprofit group that aims to protect Canadian Muslims and, through this, expand its reach to all Canadians. By encouraging civic engagement, human rights, and public advocacy this organization challenges Islamophobia and all forms of xenophobia. Through briefs, position statements, research, and outreach reports NCCM advances its mission and education.

Office of the United Nations High Commissioner for Human Rights (OHCHR)

Palais des Nations
CH-1211 Geneva 10
Switzerland
phone: 41 22 917 9220
email: InfoDesk@ohchr.org
website: www.ohchr.org/EN/Pages/Home.aspx

Mandated to guarantee global human rights, the OHCHR conducts research, identifies challenges to human rights around the globe, and also offers assistance to governments dealing with various situations. The OHCHR produces a comprehensive array of publications including fact sheets, references, training and educational manuals, and policy sheets. Their 2017 publications catalogue lists over 150 titles available in various official United Nations languages.

UN Women

220 East 42nd Street
New York, NY 10017
phone: 1-646-781-4400
fax: 1-646-781-4444
website: www.unwomen.org

UN Women, also known as the United Nations Entity for
Gender Equality and the Empowerment of Women, is a leader
in seeking equality for women, justice against discrimination, and
humanitarian rights. One of the main goals of this group is to
ensure all women the chance to develop to their full potential. This
agency is guided by several international agreements including the
UN Security Council Resolution # 1325. UN Women maintains a
digital library providing videos, multimedia, and annual reports
that document gender initiatives around the world.

Urban Institute Policy Center

2100 M Street NW
Washington, DC 20037
phone: 202-833-7200
website: www.urban.org

The Urban Institute Policy Center dedicates itself to encouraging
civic engagement, defending human rights, and public advocacy.
This organization challenges Islamophobia and all forms of
xenophobia. Through briefs, position statements, research, and
outreach reports, NCCM advances its mission and education.

Women Living Under Muslim Laws (WLUML)

PO Box 28455
London N19 5JT
United Kingdom
website: www.wluml.org

Women Living Under Muslim Laws is an international network that
provides guidance and support to women living in areas governed
by laws and customs derived from Islam. Through networking,

publications, and collective projects, WLUML works to strengthen women's equality and rights—especially in Muslim contexts. As part of this agency's educational effort they maintain a traveling exhibit titled "Dress Codes and Modes: Women's Clothing in Muslim Contexts" which identifies, explains, and educates the public about identity, morality, and autonomy relating to women's clothing.

Bibliography of Books

Lila Abu-Lughod. *Do Muslim Women Need Saving?* Cambridge, MA: Harvard University Press, 2013.

Lila Ahmed. *A Quiet Revolution: The Veil's Resurgence, From the Middle East to America.* New Haven, CT: Yale University Press, 2012.

Kecia Ali. *Sexual Ethics And Islam: Feminist Reflections on Qur'an, Hadith, and Jurisprudence.* London, UK: OneWorld, 2006

Ayaan Hirsi Ali. *The Caged Virgin: An Emancipation Proclamation for Women and Islam.* New York, NY: Free Press, 2006

Noah Berlatsky, editor. *Gendercide.* New York, NY: Greenhaven Press, 2014

Sara Blaedel. *Only One Life.* New York, NY: W.W. Norton & Co., 2011

Jimmy Carter. *A Call to Action: Women, Religion, Violence, and Power.* New York, NY: Simon & Schuster, 2014

Ayesha S. Chaudhry. *Domestic Violence and the Islamic Tradition.* Oxford, England: Oxford University Press, 2014

William Dudley, editor. *Opposing Viewpoints: Islam.* New York, NY: Greenhaven Press, 2004

Jan Goodwin. *Price of Honor: Muslim Women Lift the Veil of Silence on the Islamic World.* New York, NY: Plume, 2003

Rana Husseini. *Murder in the Name of Honor: the True Story of One Woman's Heroic Fight Against an Unbelievable Crime.* London, UK: OneWorld, 2009

Rod Nordland. *The Lovers: Afghanistan's Romeo and Juliet, the True Story of How They Defied Their Families and Escaped an Honor Killing,* New York, NY: Ecco, 2016

N. Pope. *Honor Killings in the Twenty-First Century.* London, UK: Palgrave Macmillan, 2012

Joan Wallach Scott. *The Politics of the Veil.* Princeton, NJ: Princeton University Press, 2010

Deborah Scroggins. W*anted Women: faith, lies, and the war on terror : the lives of Ayaan Hirsi Ali and Aafia Siddiqui.* New York, NY: Harper, 2012

Rae Simons with Joyce Zoldak. *Gender Danger: Survivors of Rape, Human Trafficking, and Honor Killings.* Broomall, PA: Mason Crest Publishers, 2009.

Souad in collaboration with Marie-Therese Cuny. *Burned Alive: a Victim of the Law of Men.* New York, NY: Warner Books, 2004.

Katherine Zoepf. *Excellent Daughters: The Secret Lives of Young Women Who Are Transforming the Arab World,* New York, NY: Penguin Press, 2016

Index